Contracts for Couples

Contracts for Couples

Alison Sawyer, BA, LLB

Self-Counsel Press
(a division of)
International Self-Counsel Press Ltd.
Canada USA

Self-Counsel Press acknowledges the financial support of the Government of Canada through the Book Publishing Industry Development Program (BPIDP) for our publishing activities.

Printed in Canada.

First edition: 2003

Canadian Cataloguing in Publication Data

Sawyer, Alison, 1948 —
Contracts for couples / Alison Sawyer.

(Self-counsel legal series)
ISBN 1-55180-387-9

1. Antenuptial contracts—Canada—Popualr works. I. Title. II. Series.
KE559.S28 2003 346.7101'6 C2002-911518-3 KF529.S28 2003

Thanks to Ruth Lea Taylor, the creator of the original drafts of the Cohabitation/Prenuptial/Marriage Agreement and the Cohabitation Agreement for Same-Sex Couples used in this book.

Jointly Acquired Asset Agreement and Separately Acquired Asset Agreement originated by Heather Fayers for Self-Counsel Press.

Self-Counsel Press
(a division of)
International Self-Counsel Press Ltd.

1481 Charlotte Road
North Vancouver, BC V7J 1H1
Canada

1704 N. State Street
Bellingham, WA 98225
USA

Contents

Table

Checklist

Notice to Readers

Laws are constantly changing. Every effort is made to keep this publication as current as possible. However, the author, the publisher, and the vendor of this book make no representation or warranties regarding the outcome or the use to which the information in this book is put and are not assuming any liability for any claims, losses, or damages arising out of the use of this book. The reader should not rely on the author or the publisher of this book for any professional advice. Please be sure that you have the most recent edition.

In creating an agreement for a situation in which large assets are involved, or if one spouse's income is substantially higher than the other, or for situations in which one spouse will be supporting the other during the term of their cohabitation, a lawyer should be consulted.

Introduction

This book is a guide for couples who want to draft their own prenuptial, marriage, or cohabitation agreements. The first chapter functions as an introduction to the various types of domestic agreements, and the second chapter deals with some essential characteristics of the agreements themselves. Chapters three and four examine what can be covered in legal agreements. The final chapter sets out some of the practical aspects of drafting a contract. The last portion of the book is a collection of sample agreements, which you can use as models for drafting your own agreement, and some blanks.

This kit is intended to be used as a working tool for you to reach your own decision about your relationship. It is not intended to be applied without thought to your particular situation. You are expected to read it over carefully, discuss it, and adapt it as necessary to suit your expectations. Do not be afraid to change the contracts. Cross out any items in the contracts provided that do not apply to your situation and initial the deletion. If there are a number of deletions and alterations on one page, it might be a good idea to retype that whole page and make the necessary number of photocopies. If you are using the computer disk included in this edition, simply delete the items you don't want and print out the necessary number of copies. We suggest couples review both the Cohabitation/Prenuptial/Marriage Agreement and the Cohabitation Agreement for Same-Sex Spouses to see alternative ways in which disposition of property and the issue of separation may be treated.

Part One
CONTRACTS FOR COUPLES

1

The What, Why, Who, When, and Where of Contracts

1. What Is a Domestic Contract?

A domestic contract (prenuptial, marriage, or cohabitation) is an agreement negotiated between both members of a couple. It deals with various aspects of their relationship, and clearly states how these matters will be handled during cohabitation as well as in the event that the couple separate. The agreement is set out in written form, signed by each of the parties, and witnessed. At that point, any oral agreements between the parties are replaced by those they have put in writing.

A relationship can be defined as a domestic partnership, whether the couple are married or living as common-law or as same-sex partners. (The word "spouses" is now used in many types of provincial and federal legislation to cover all couples.) Now that the legal differences between married and unmarried and between heterosexual and same-sex partnerships are dissolving, there are really only two different kinds of domestic contracts: those made by people who plan to live together or who are living together, and those made at the time of separation or after the breakdown of the relationship. The latter are always simply called "separation agreements." The former are called marriage contracts, prenuptial contracts, cohabitation agreements, or domestic contracts or agreements.

A domestic agreement may be written subsequent to marriage or cohabitation. It may also be written before the marriage or before cohabitation begins, as long as the agreement is stated to be "in contemplation of marriage" or "in anticipation of living together." No domestic agreement can include a term by which the parties agreeing to divorce (for married couples) as a result of certain events or at a particular time. Only a court can dissolve a marriage.

Example

Jacqui and Linda began living together one year ago. They are now both living in Linda's condominium and have been saving to buy a van. They have decided that they will put the van in Jacqui's name, even though they will both be contributing to its purchase.

They have decided to write an agreement that will formalize the system they have worked out for tracking their financial contributions to the household and their assets. They also want their agreement to specify the method to which they have both consented for dividing all their property in the event their relationship doesn't last. The agreement they are going to write is called a cohabitation agreement or a living-together contract. If a legally married couple want to write the same kind of agreement, it would be called a marriage agreement or a marriage contract.

If a couple makes an oral agreement, but does not put it into writing, the agreement may nonetheless be legally binding. However, oral agreements are difficult to enforce, largely because there are usually evidentiary issues (i.e., there may be no solid evidence as to the substance of the agreement, giving rise to the problem of whom to believe in a dispute). For this reason, lawyers are reluctant to attempt to enforce oral agreements through the courts, and encourage people to put their agreements in writing.

Example

After living together for five years, Al and Sara broke up. Sara had been attending university to get a PhD, and Al had been helping her by buying a car for her and making payments on it. The car was in his name because the loan was in his name, and they had agreed verbally that he would make the payments until she was finished her schooling. Al also agreed that if they broke up before Sara got her degree, he would put the car in her name. At the time of these agreements, neither Al nor Sara could imagine that they would ever split up.

They parted company, however, when Sara was within a year of finishing her schooling. She had no more classes to take, but still had to finish her research project and write her thesis. Al moved out and took the car with him. When Sara reminded him of his promise to give her the car, he said he had been letting her use it only until she had finished her classes.

That was not the way Sara remembered the agreement. Nonetheless, if Sara attempted to enforce the agreement, she would have only her word against his that he had promised to put the car in her name. There is no rule in law for couples who are not married that property (even property held in the name of one spouse only) is jointly owned. If Sara couldn't persuade Al to transfer the registration, her only recourse would be to sue him for breach of trust (explained below) and for spousal support (which is allowed between common-law spouses) as an alternative form of compensation.

An agreement may cover anything the parties wish it to cover, but it will not be enforceable through the legal system if the agreement is about trivial or illegal matters. (For example, you can't have a legally binding agreement about how to defraud the credit-card company.) There is a variety of other factors that can make a contract unenforceable or void, such as duress or misrepresentation by either party of the terms or facts involved. These problems will be discussed in the next chapter, but be aware that the law will not enforce provisions that deal with household roles and responsibilities (e.g., who does what housework), because these matters are not defined in law. There is no law on the subject of household roles and responsibilities.

Example

Gary and Mai were legally married. Mai worked in a car dealership, where she was the only female employee. Shortly after the wedding, Gary became very jealous of her. He wrote up an agreement that included as one of its terms that Mai must be at home within one hour of finishing work. He included an additional term that she was to have sexual relations with him no fewer than three times a week. The agreement Gary drafted also stated that if Mai didn't obey these terms, he would divorce her and wouldn't pay her any spousal support if they separated.

Mai signed the paper because she did not want him to leave her. But then she took the agreement to a lawyer. The lawyer told her the agreement could not be enforced, not only because she was given no choice in signing it (she had been afraid Gary would end their marriage if she didn't sign) but also because the terms were not such that a court would uphold. Furthermore, the lawyer told her that regardless of whether or not she followed the terms of the agreement, Gary would not be able to divorce her without filing for the divorce in court, and that the only legal grounds for divorce were adultery, cruelty, or separation for one year or more.

The rules of form and content that make a domestic contract legal are covered in part by the family law legislation in each province, but contract law (as developed for commercial purposes) also applies. Rules for drafting and interpreting contracts have been developed over centuries of commercial transactions, and the problems mentioned above that make a contract unenforceable were first identified in commercial law. When a cohabitation agreement has to be enforced through the courts, the judge will look both at family legislation and at contract law.

2. Who Can Be a Party to a Domestic Contract?

Until recently, married couples, by virtue of getting a marriage licence and going through the ceremony of marriage, had mutual obligations towards each other that were not assumed to be inherent in common-law or same-sex partnerships. For example, it is implicit in the marriage vows that each partner is responsible for the maintenance of the other. Even though Gary, in the example above, had included in his agreement with Mai that he would not support her if the marriage ended, the court would nonetheless consider a request from Mai for spousal support. The court would look at financial need and at the overall fairness of the contract, including the fact that Mai had no choice but to sign it.

Now, however, the courts and statutes of most provinces (see Table 1: Provincial Legislation at the end of this chapter) assign to any kind of long-term living-together relationship many of the same obligations inherent in a marriage (e.g., one's obligation, after the relationship ends, to provide support to the needy spouse or to the children, even if one is not the biological parent). These obligations are binding on non-married (common-law) couples (and, in many provinces, on same-sex couples) who have lived together from one to five years, depending on which government and which statute governs. The only way a couple can alter or change the nature of the obligation is by entering into a fair written agreement or by obtaining a court order.

Marital property legislation does not yet apply to common-law and same-sex couples, so it is particularly important for people who have such arrangements to create a written agreement regarding all their property. If property is not held jointly (i.e., in both names), it may be difficult to divide it fairly upon separation, because between unmarried couples, property is often presumed to be wholly owned by the person whose name is on the title, regardless of financial or other contributions to the purchase and upkeep of that property. That is why, in the earlier example, Sara is going to have trouble getting the car Al had promised her.

3. Why Enter into a Domestic Contract?

Whether spouses make long-term plans or not, they tend to conduct their affairs as if they were never going to separate. Household goods are merged, and there may be a joint bank account for running the home, but often no clear statement exists regarding who is responsible for which expenses. There may be children from a previous relationship, and the non-biological parent may not be clear about the nature of his or her obligation or the expectations of his or her partner. Furthermore, there are some spouses who may have differing ideas about whether or not the relationship will eventually include children. Property may have been brought into the relationship or acquired during the relationship by inheritance, but there may be no clear statement regarding ownership.

As a result, when the domestic partnership breaks down, there are often a number of loose ends. In the above example of Jacqui and Linda, Jacqui assumed that the strata property would be Linda's on separation. It had remained in Linda's name, as it had been hers before they got together. However, Jacqui made financial contributions toward the property. If Jacqui and Linda hadn't written a cohabitation agreement, Jacqui, in the event of a breakup, might face a battle with Linda to recover at least the value of her own contributions to the property.

The most common and important issues are —

- how both the separate and jointly owned property will be divided upon breakdown; and
- custody of, access to, and support of children.

(Note, however, that under the laws of certain provinces [i.e, New Brunswick, Newfoundland, Nunavut, Ontario, Prince Edward Island, and Yukon] these issues cannot be covered in cohabitation agreements. In other provinces [i.e., Alberta, Nova Scotia, British Columbia], any terms regarding custody of, access to, and support of children may be disregarded by the courts.) Some people also want to cover the eventuality of death, but a legal will is a much more effective instrument for that purpose.

Creating a written agreement before the relationship breaks down or, better yet, at the time cohabitation begins means that both parties have discussed and come to some accord about important issues. If a judge has to decide any of these matters, the results may be very different from what the couple would wish. Another advantage of entering into a written agreement is that the psychological and economic expectations each party has of the other — as well as of the relationship itself — will be aired during the negotiation, resulting, one hopes, in a measure of clarity once the agreement is signed.

For some people, these discussions are more important than finalizing a legally binding contract. Furthermore, it may be that the couple decides that the law of their province is already appropriate for their situation and sees no reason to change how the law applies to them. Alternatively, the couple may recognize that they have no property to divide at the outset of their relationship and no way of reliably predicting what property they will accumulate during their relationship. In such a case, it is appropriate to leave negotiating an agreement to a time when there is significant property. Couples contemplating acquiring assets jointly may want to review Sample 3: Jointly Acquired Asset Agreement (in the Sample section of this book). If one person in the relationship would like to separately acquire an asset, see Sample 4: Separately Acquired Asset Agreement.

Married couples who cannot settle their affairs upon separation are covered by their provincial marital property laws. These laws are aimed at equalizing the division of marital property between the separating husband and wife. If the couple does not want their property to be equalized upon separation, the ownership rights must be set down in a contract. (These laws will be discussed in a later chapter.)

The main difference that arises from being legally married as opposed to living common law is that the family law rules about division of marital property apply to ensure an equal division of family assets. At present these rules do not apply to non-married couples. However, if a cohabitation or separation agreement deals with property issues, most provinces will allow enforcement of the agreement through the courts. If a domestic contract has been filed with the superior court by common-law or same-sex partners, a judge may decide a disputed case using the same laws that apply to married couples. If an agreement has been written but has not been filed and the courts are asked to enforce it, a judge will apply the law of trusts and equity — law made by judges rather than by the provincial legislature. The judge will attempt to decide if property has been gifted and whether or not there have been direct contributions by one party to property owned by the other. Same-sex couples may wish to review Sample 2: Cohabitation Agreement for Same-Sex Couples (in the Sample section).

Example

According to their agreement, Jacqui and Linda each pay $800 per month into their joint account to cover household utility bills, car payments, insurance (for the new van), household insurance, and property taxes. They also set out in their agreement that Linda pays for her own car, which she had obtained before she and Jacqui got together. Linda will not share the value of her car with Jacqui if they split up, but they agree to share the value of the van because Linda has decided that she wants Jacqui to have half the fair market value of the condominium if they separate. All this is set out in the agreement, along with their decision on division of their pensions and RRSPs.

As long as both members of the couple sign the agreement, the agreement will be legally binding (subject to the rules regarding form and content discussed in Chapter 2). If one party fails to abide by the terms of the agreement, the other party can start a court action to enforce it. Alternatively, the contract may specify that disputes about implementation and enforcement of the agreement be resolved by mediation or arbitration, as agreed by the parties. Court would be the final option if all other attempts to settle the problem fail.

4. When Should an Agreement Be Made?

Most people who are newly in love and just starting to live together do not see the need for a contract. Indeed, they often find the idea of negotiating one repugnant because the process is contrary to the notions of trust and faith held by lovers. To negotiate the terms of a cohabitation agreement, one of the partners first has to broach the idea that a contract might be desirable. To have a discussion about it means that the couple must think and talk about issues such as ownership of property, division of income and expenses in the relationship, children, and the possibility of separation. For a couple to come to grips with the issues realistically also means that each party must disclose to the other his or her income, debts and other liabilities (for example, payment of child support), and property and business holdings, including savings, insurance policies, and RRSPs.

In some cases, details of past relationships, spending habits (and present debt load), or future plans with regard to children have not been made manifest during a couple's courtship period. Lawyers argue that a discussion of the terms of a cohabitation agreement can create an opportunity for dealing with unpleasant surprises at the beginning of a couple's relationship, when such surprises stand a chance of being incorporated into the relationship, or, alternatively, may lead to its early demise, which may be just as well. Unfortunately, most people feel that ignorance is bliss, and so do not create any cohabitation agreement.

So it is not often that a written agreement will be created at the outset of a domestic partnership, although lawyers highly recommend doing so, particularly if either member of the couple owns significant property. However, when an agreement is created, it usually covers the status of property in the name of one or the other party during and after the relationship (as in the example of Jacqui and Linda, above). The couple may make provision in their agreement for the payment of support in the event of separation. Such agreements sometimes include terms regarding the domestic duties and the responsibilities of each party. If there are children involved, or if there is an expectation of having children, a couple's agreement may deal with various aspects of the education, moral training, and support during the relationship, as well as custody and access in the event of separation. (Once again note, however, that some provinces curtail such provisions. See section **3.** above.)

Of course, as discussed in the previous section, there may not be much point in having an agreement at a time in the relationship when there is no property and there are no issues around the having and raising of children. A cohabitation agreement can be created at any time during the relationship. Nor does an agreement have to cover all aspects of cohabitating. It may be more appropriate to enter into an agreement for a specific purpose, such as upon the acquisition of a major asset (for example, when the couple decides to buy a home or start a business).

Example

Linda and Jacqui had both been in so-called long-term relationships before. They had learned the hard way that they could not rely on the legal system to settle their disputes. They were therefore willing to negotiate a written cohabitation agreement to deal with their property. As part of their discussions regarding Linda's proposal to give Jacqui a half-interest in her condominium upon separation, they disclosed to each other the details of their incomes, their savings, and their pensions. Although each knew the type of work the other did, and the names of their respective employers, they had never discussed their overall financial situations.

Linda, in particular, found it difficult to give Jacqui all the information, because she knew that she probably had more savings. Jacqui was still paying off her substantial student loans and was less frugal than Linda. Linda had always had a desire to feel secure financially and so was careful about saving. She didn't want Jacqui to feel that she, Linda, was being charitable towards her.

In the end, they decided they would each produce for the other their bank statements as well as their income-tax assessments and returns for the past three years. Jacqui had to remind Linda about her promise to do so for two or three weeks before Linda complied. It was only then that they finished their discussion about setting up a joint account to handle the household finances and to pay for the new van. They attached to their written agreement copies of the information that they had produced for each other.

Separation agreements made when a partnership fails are more common than cohabitation agreements. There are far fewer unknowns at the time of separation than at the outset of cohabitation.

The couple wants clarity on how the property, including pensions and money in the bank, will be divided and what must be done with the debt. If there are children, each party will want to plan for their care, including the payment of support.

At this point, the lack of trust and the problems in a relationship may make it difficult to negotiate a written separation agreement. If the parties know each other's personalities well enough and are satisfied that an oral promise will result in the regular payment of support, that may be the extent of the agreement. An oral agreement regarding the payment of child support or the division of the debt load may be enforceable, especially if some payments have been made.

5. Where, or under Which Law?

As mentioned above, the property regimes in the provincial statutes still apply only to legally married couples. Federal income-tax and pension law have now been changed to include common-law and same-sex partners, so agreements can provide for pension and credit splitting. But the division of other property held by one member of a same-sex or common-law couple in his or her own name is decided by trust law and equity. An investigation must be made of the facts surrounding the parties' intentions at the time cohabitation began or when the property was acquired, whether one party made a gift of the property to the other, and whether declarations were made to others outside the couple about the ownership or right of possession of the party who is not on title.

Example

Sara had always understood that Al was making a gift of the car to her even though his name was down as the registered owner. She could support her argument in a court case by showing that Al never drove the car, as he had his own. He drove a pick-up truck but had bought her a pale-blue Volkswagen with a customized pink interior. Sara could argue that given Al's tastes, it was unlikely that he would want a car such as the one he had bought her. She could also call as witnesses those friends and relatives who had heard Al talk about having bought Sara a car.

An agreement made in one province can deal with the disposition of a couple's property, regardless of where the property is situated. However, the agreement should specify which province's law applies if enforcement in court is necessary. Usually, it is the law of the province in which the parties are resident. If the agreement doesn't specify which province's laws apply, enforcement becomes difficult, as the presumption is that the law of the province in which the party is bringing the action applies. Some provinces set out rules about which law to apply when there is property in more than one province or country. If you find yourself in this situation, you would be wise to consult a lawyer.

TABLE 1
PROVINCIAL LEGISLATION

Leg.	BC	AB	SK	MB	ON	NB	NS	PEI	NFL	YK
Domestic Contract	No	No	Yes	No	Yes	Yes	Yes	Yes	Yes	Yes
Marriage Contract	Yes	Yes	Same	Yes	Yes	Yes	Yes	No	Yes	Yes
Independent Legal Advice	No	Yes	Yes	No	No	Yes	No	No	Yes	No
Disclosure	Yes	No	No	Yes	Yes	Yes	No	Yes	No	Yes
Provision for Filing	Yes	No	No	Yes	Yes	No	Yes	Yes	Yes	No
Same-sex Definition	Yes	No	Yes	Yes	Yes	No	Yes	No	Yes	No
# yrs	2	3	2	2	3	3	3	2	2	3

Domestic contract: Term Domestic Contracts used in the legislation to apply to more (or less, depending on your point of view) than married

Marriage Contract: Only for married couples

Independent Legal Advice: Necessary for contract to be valid

Disclosure: Disclosure of property, etc., a requirement for a valid contract

Provision for filing: Provision for filing agreement with the superior court for enforcement purposes

Same-sex Definition: Definition of same-sex relationships included with common-law definition

yrs: Number of years same-sex/common-law relationship must exist to be covered by the legislation

2
Basic Legal Requirements

There are several requirements that any contract must meet in order for that contract to be legal and enforceable. This chapter will give you information on how to ensure that the language and content of your contract are adequate, and will discuss several factors that may work to render your contract invalid.

1. Mutual Promises or an Exchange for Value

The first rule of contract law is that there must be an exchange of something of value to bind the agreement. One party to the agreement must agree to give something of value or give up something of value in exchange for what the other party has promised to give or to do or to give up or not to do. For example, in the purchase of property, the property is sold in return for an agreed amount of money. The money is called, in legal terms, the "consideration" for the contract. The law, however, does not question the amount of the consideration. It requires only that there be some consideration.

In a domestic contract, the consideration is said to be "good" (meaning something of value) if the agreement is expressed as being based on the exchange of promises set out in the agreement. An exchange of promises explicitly stated in the agreement is usually sufficient, but if the terms of the agreement appear to set out a one-sided bargain, something more is required. In such a case, a specific statement that the agreement is based on "mutual love and affection" strengthens the consideration. Generally, to strengthen your domestic contract it is a good idea to specifically state that the consideration is based on mutual love and affection.

Example

A cohabitation agreement drafted by lawyers might deal with consideration in this way:

"In consideration of the promises and mutual covenants contained in this agreement, the parties agree as follows. . . ."

The same statement can be put in slightly simpler language:

"In consideration of the mutual promises contained in this agreement, we agree to be bound by the following terms. . . ." OR, "In consideration of the mutual love and affection that exists between the parties, we agree to be bound by the following terms. . . ."

2. Contract Language

A contract must be specific in its language. This requirement springs from the nature of contracts themselves. A contract sets out terms that by mutual agreement will be binding on both parties to the contract. Some terms are to be followed by one person; some by another. If one of the parties doesn't follow the terms of the contract, the other party can enforce the contract. That person doesn't want the first party's defence to be that the term wasn't clear. For example, take the case of Gary and Mai. If all the contract were to say on the subject of support payments was "Support payments are to be made by Gary to Mai," Gary could say he didn't have to make payments, because the amount and time of payment weren't specified. A judge would agree with him. The language must be specific. The following is an example of the kind of exact language you must use:

Example

"Support payments are to be made by Gary to Mai in the amount of $500.00 per month, payable on the 1st of every month and beginning on the 1st of the month immediately following the signing of this agreement. These monthly payments are to continue until the occurrence of one of the following events: Mai begins to earn more than $1,800.00 gross per month, Mai remarries, or three years have passed from the date of this agreement."

Similarly, a term stating, "The family home will be sold and the money will be divided between the parties" will not be effective. Again, no time has been specified for when the house is to be put on the market, nor is an asking price set out, nor is it made clear what money will be divided and in what proportions.

These are extreme examples, but a failure to specify the details of a contract's terms is a common characteristic of agreements drafted by non-lawyers. It is true that making the language more specific and more detailed means the paragraphs will be longer. The trick is to express each detail simply, so that anyone can see its meaning. If the meaning is not clear, the term may not be enforceable, and therefore the provision for support or for sale of the home will not be effective. (See Chapter 5 for more information on contract language.)

3. Sealing the Bargain or Signing the Agreement

It is surprising how many people think that it is the negotiating and then committing of terms to paper that make an agreement. While it is true that writing the terms on paper is significant, *the paper is not a legally binding and enforceable contract until both parties have signed it and the signatures have been witnessed.* It is therefore a specified requirement in all provincial family law statutes that domestic contracts be in writing, signed by both parties, and that both signatures must be witnessed.

Domestic agreements are not sworn documents; that is, they are not signed under oath. However, they are enforceable contracts. By signing in front of witnesses, the signors are confirming that they will be bound to keep and abide by the terms and promises that are the subject matter of the agreement.

4. Fairness

In determining the enforceability of domestic contracts, fairness is a key consideration. Fairness is an issue both with regard to the terms that were negotiated as well as the bargaining position of the parties during the negotiation.

Fairness of bargaining position is particularly important when dealing with couples. For a variety of reasons, there is often an economic or status disparity between the two parties; as, for example, in the case of Linda and Jacqui in the previous chapter. In that instance, the partners handled the disparity in their respective financial situations by making full disclosure to each other of the details of their financial situations, backed up by documentary records.

Although it is most common these days for both members of a couple to work, often one partner has a greater income than the other. Women continue to earn less, on average, than do men. When there are children, women are frequently the primary caregivers. But regardless of which spouse has primary responsibility for raising the children, that person's work outside the home is often only part-time and, therefore, less lucrative. And the caregiver, with or without work, is often considered to have less status than the partner working full-time.

When such disparities exist, fairness in the bargaining process is often an issue. To ensure fairness, independent legal advice must be obtained before the agreement is signed.

There are a few criteria for assessing whether the negotiating of a cohabitation or separation agreement was done fairly. One important factor is disclosure; another is independent legal advice. These factors are explained next.

5. Disclosure

Each party must disclose his or her financial position to the other. Under family law, fair terms cannot be negotiated if one party is withholding information about his or her assets or income. Lawyers ask the parties to exchange completed property and financial statements, which must be sworn in front of a lawyer or a notary and accompanied by three years' worth of income-tax returns, recent pay stubs, and recent bank statements.

These statements require disclosure of all assets held (and their value), including pensions, insurance policies, savings, real estate, jewellery, vehicles, and business investments, as well as regular monthly income and expenses. Expenses would include support payments to former spouses or children from previous relationships and interest payments on mortgages and other types of debts, such as personal loans and credit cards. (See Schedule A and Schedule B attached to Sample 1: Cohabitation/Prenuptial/Marriage Agreement in the Samples section of this book.)

It is surprising how many people are reluctant to divulge their exact worth even to their partners or partners-to-be. The partner who is in the inferior position is often reluctant to make a point of wanting to know the other's finances. This is especially true at the beginning of the partnership, when trust is assumed to be implicit and any request for information that has not already been freely offered can be construed as demonstrating a lack of trust, or worse, greed.

However, if, sometime after cohabitation has begun, a couple negotiate an agreement (prompted, for example, by the imminent purchase of real estate), full financial disclosure is perhaps easier to obtain. In most cases, people who have been living together for a period of time are aware of the other person's income, debts, and financial responsibilities. It is then much easier to reveal the actual details or, at least, it is easier to question the other person and be reasonably satisfied with the answers.

For those people who have no idea of their partner's finances even after living with that person for an extended period, financial disclosure is especially important. People who are secretive about their money may be reluctant to share, or it may be that they are not presenting an honest picture of their situations. It is not unheard of for a spouse to be under the impression that his or her partner is earning $2,500 a month, when in fact the income is $3,000 a month with $500 going from source into a RRSP. That RRSP should be declared on the financial statement by that spouse and taken into account. It may not be, if the other spouse doesn't ask to see pay stubs.

In any event, it is a good idea to find out everything so that issues can be dealt with fairly — issues such as how to own the property, how to deal with debt, and any need for financial support. Failure to receive adequate disclosure is often a ground for invalidating an agreement. For this reason, you should include in your agreement a term acknowledging that disclosure was made and describing the nature or type of disclosure.

6. Independent Legal Advice

The obligation to get independent legal advice is another criterion of a fair agreement. If an agreement breaks down and is reviewed by a judge, the judge will want to know if both parties received independent legal advice. Receiving independent legal advice means that each party, prior to signing the agreement, reviewed its terms with his or her own separately retained lawyer (one whom he or she chose and for which he or she paid).

When drafting cohabitation or separation agreements, most lawyers will either include a paragraph stating that each party was informed of the need for legal advice or will attach a Certificate of Independent Legal Advice for one party to take to another lawyer. *It is unethical for lawyers to witness the signatures of both parties to an agreement.* Instead, the lawyer who drafted the agreement will require the party who did not retain him or her to have a consultation with a second lawyer, who will witness that person's signature.

Even if a couple consults a lawyer together about entering into a domestic contract, that lawyer will require one of the parties to see another lawyer, either during the drafting process or at the time of signing. That way, each party will have received separate advice about the law that applies to his or her situation and will be able to have a frank and independent discussion about the fairness of the bargain for him or her.

Often, when one member of a couple is in a weaker position or is more emotional than practical, that person will say, "Oh I'll sign whatever." His or her lawyer then has the task of explaining what that party's full entitlement is in law and must counsel that party on which bargaining strategy might work for his or her situation. Of course, the client is not bound to take the advice and may choose to go along with what the lawyer has said is a bad deal. The lawyer can still sign a Certificate of Independent Legal Advice or witness the client's signature to an agreement stating that that party has had an opportunity to consult a lawyer. The lawyer may also include a statement that the client failed to take the advice offered.

Perhaps if Sara had asked a lawyer if she would have any trouble getting title to the car when Al bought it as a gift for her, she would have realized that Al and the bank could have entered into a loan agreement concerning the car, even with her name on the car registration. Or she could have had Al sign a note agreeing to the terms by which he would hand over title to the car to Sara.

7. Grounds for Setting aside the Whole Agreement

A judge may set aside an entire agreement as being unfair if duress, undue influence, unconscionability, or fraud are found to have been factored into the negotiation process. Any one of these factors can render an agreement unenforceable.

7.1 Duress

If one spouse uses physical violence or threatens violence or imprisonment (forcible confinement) to persuade the other to sign the agreement, duress is deemed to have occurred. Any contract that is discovered to have been signed after an assault or the threat of an assault will mostly likely be declared invalid. In such circumstances, the victim cannot have, as he or she must, freely consented to the agreement. However, the victim must try to have the agreement revoked as soon as possible following the assault or threat, rather than waiting until the other party tries to enforce the contract.

Economic duress may also be grounds for setting aside an agreement. This ground requires the agreement to have been signed as a result of immediately pressing and unavoidable economic troubles.

Economic duress can be hard to prove. A judge will need evidence that coercion occurred, that there was no alternative course of action, and that the victim had not been independently advised.

7.2 Material misrepresentation or fraud

If the financial or property information disclosed was not complete or current at the time the agreement was signed or was false or misleading on important items, the agreement can be set aside. Such would be the case if, say, an RRSP account was not disclosed. If intention to misrepresent or hide information can be shown (that is, if a spouse was proven to have lied), then there is a presumption of fraud.

7.3 Unconscionability

An agreement will not be valid if it can be shown that one party held out inducements to persuade the other party to sign; such as, in the case of a separation agreement, "allowing" the other party to have sole custody of the children in exchange for clear title to his or her half of the matrimonial home. Alternatively, if the stronger party takes advantage of the other's weaknesses to extract a grossly unfair bargain, the agreement may be set aside, as in the case of the higher-income earner demanding full title to the matrimonial home in exchange for the payment of a minimal amount of support. The party benefitting must be able to show that the bargain was fair, just, and reasonable; in other words, that no advantage was taken.

7.4 Undue influence

If the terms of the agreement are so harsh as to be unjust, the party suffering thereby may allege that the other party knew that he or she was in a vulnerable state and used scare tactics to obtain his or her consent to the agreement. The question is not one of mental capacity but rather the process by which the decision to sign the agreement was reached. However, undue influence cannot be proved if the influenced party received independent legal advice. There can be no undue influence if it can be shown that the person alleging so made the agreement as a result of free, full, and informed consent.

7.5 Mistake

Mistake is another factor that can render an agreement (either whole or in part) unenforceable. Mistake arises when the understanding that formed the basis of the agreement was not mutual. Common mistakes are with respect to the nature of the subject matter of the agreement or its terms or the nature of the legal title to the property and its quality. The assumptions upon which the agreement was made may have been fundamentally wrong in the mind of one or both spouses. For example, a contract could be altered if a recreational property was left out of the terms, even though it had been part of the negotiations. Alternatively, if one party grossly underestimated the value of a pension, any term dealing with that pension could be rendered void by a court and, thus, re-negotiated.

3
The Content of an Agreement

This book deals only with domestic contracts (prenuptial, marriage, or cohabitation agreements), although by and large, the same rules and laws apply to separation agreements. Obviously, the process of separation puts the parties in a different relationship to each other; therefore, separation agreements have a different focus from cohabitation agreements.

When negotiating an agreement before or during cohabitation, the primary focus will most likely be the ownership of property and the handling of household finances, with the secondary focus being the issues that are likely to arise if the relationship fails. You will want the focus to be on property and finances if you or your spouse has real estate, a family business, or substantial savings (which would include RRSPS or a pension plan). This type of property is covered by provincial family (marital) legislation. By entering into a cohabitation agreement, you are avoiding the application of provincial law to the property covered in your agreement (which is the reason many people choose to negotiate a cohabitation agreement, as mentioned in the first chapter). Remember, though, that provincial legislation sets out which topics the law considers appropriate for cohabitation and marriage agreements. In most provinces, as discussed in Chapter 1, both marriage and cohabitation agreements can cover the following topics:

(a) Ownership in or division of property

(b) Support obligations

(c) The right to direct the education and moral training of the parties' children, but not the right to custody of or access to their children

(d) Any other matter in the settlement of the parties' affairs

In addition, you should be aware that if a cohabitation agreement deals with property, it can be filed with the courts in some provinces (British Columbia, Manitoba, Nova Scotia, Newfoundland, and Ontario) for the purpose of enforcement as a court order using the rules of the family law legislation, just as when a marriage agreement is enforced. This makes taking the defaulting spouse to court much simpler. In the other provinces and territories, a cohabitation agreement could be enforced through a lawsuit using contract and trust law. If you live in a province in which agreements can be filed in court for purposes of enforcement and you choose not to file one, or if you live in a province in which the law does not allow you to file one, you can nonetheless use the written agreement as evidence in any lawsuit you bring to enforce its provisions should there be a breach of the agreement (such as failure to pay support).

Spousal support may also be covered in a domestic contract. Finally, a couple may want to use their agreement to do some estate planning. These topics will be discussed later in this chapter.

1. Property

In family law, the rules about matrimonial property apply only to legally married couples (except in Saskatchewan). There have been at least two cases started in provincial superior courts to extend the property laws to common-law and same-sex couples, but these cases will take another two or three years to reach the Supreme Court of Canada. In the meantime, most provinces take the position that family or marital property law applies only to married couples. For this reason, this chapter discusses the law for married couples in section **2.** and the law for common-law and same-sex partners in section **3.**

2. Marital Property Law

The law for married couples changed in the 1970s to allow both spouses to benefit from any accumulation of assets during the marriage. Prior to this change, only the spouse in whose name property was held would keep that property if the marriage failed. If the other spouse had made financial contributions to help buy or to maintain the property, he or she would get only the value of those contributions from the owning spouse, and that only by launching an expensive court case. The law that applied was the law of trusts and unjust enrichment, which is the law that common-law and same-sex partners are using still. (See the example of Al, Sarah, and the car, discussed in Chapters 1 and 2.)

Provincial family legislation now gives a definition of marital property (or family property, as it is called in some provinces) that is to be divided equally upon separation and (in some provinces) lists exempted property. (See below for more explanation.) Property that is exempted will remain the property of the person with title (legal ownership) after separation. The legislation also sets out the factors (i.e., the length of the marriage, the relative contributions of the spouses to the household, the nature of the property) a judge can apply to divide the property in any way other than a 50-50 split.

What does this legislation mean to married couples? Simply this: those who do not want to share their property equally upon separation or who want to share equally property that is exempted under the law must make a written agreement, and that agreement must detail how the couple wants the property held during the relationship and how they want it to be divided upon separation. (See the example of Jacqui and Linda in Chapters 1 and 2). If a marriage contract exists between the couple, the court will uphold its terms with regard to division of property, as long as the parties entered into the contract fairly and the agreement meets the requirements for a valid contract as discussed in Chapter 2.

2.1 What is marital property?

A marriage agreement, as was explained in Chapter 1, is much the same as a cohabitation agreement, except that there is a statutory definition of marriage agreements in provincial law restricting marriage agreements to contracts between legally married couples who wish to deal with ownership of property by written agreement. If the formal requirements for a marriage agreement as set out in provincial law are met, then the agreement, as discussed above, can be used to avoid the application of statutory rules for division of marital property upon marriage breakdown. The agreement can be made in contemplation of marriage (that is, before the marriage takes place), or it can be entered into after marriage. In either case, as long as it contains terms regarding ownership of property and is in writing, signed by both parties, and witnessed, the agreement is properly called a marriage agreement.

Before you draft an agreement dealing with property, you should know what the provincial law defines as family or marital (or matrimonial) property. For example, you should know that both real property (land, or land and buildings) and personal property (e.g., household goods, jewellery, and cash) are included, so you should cover these in your agreement. To the extent that you cover your property in an agreement, the provincial law will not apply. Similarly, property you hold in joint title with your spouse, such as real estate or joint bank accounts, is not covered by marital property law.

Some examples of family (marital) property are —

- the marital home;
- household furniture;
- the family car;
- a summer cottage;
- money in savings, chequing, or current accounts (if this money is used for family purposes);
- rights under life insurance policies, or accident and sickness insurance policies, or annuity policies;
- pensions; and
- registered retirement savings plans (RRSPs).

When you think about what property to include in a marriage agreement, you will probably start by thinking about whatever property issue motivated you to want to draft an agreement. You may, for instance, have a recreational property that has been passed down in your family and which you want to keep in your family. Or you may be about to invest in a business and want to ensure that your spouse does not acquire a right to share in it or its profits. But when you ask your spouse to sign such an agreement, you may find that he or she wants to negotiate terms covering all assets owned by the two of you, since fairness requires some give and take.

There are two different systems for dividing marital property. The first, used by some provinces, is a deferred community-property system or a system of equal entitlement upon separation. The community property is marital property; that is, property that is used for a family purpose, such as shelter, transportation, or recreation, during the time the parties are married and living together. The second system, used by other provinces, is an equalization scheme: in addition to using the concept of family property, the legislation states that all property owned by the spouses from the time of marriage to the date of separation must be valued upon separation. (Each province has a different rule about the date of valuation. Usually it is the date of separation or divorce.) The difference between the value of the property owned by the husband and the value of the property owned by the wife is calculated and divided in a 50-50 split. Both schemes allow for some property to be exempted from the calculations.

Provinces and territories with an equal-entitlement system are as follows:

- British Columbia
- New Brunswick
- Newfoundland
- Nova Scotia
- Saskatchewan
- Yukon

Provinces and territories with an equalization system are as follows:

- Alberta
- Manitoba
- Ontario
- Prince Edward Island
- Northwest Territories
- Nunavut

Some examples of property exempted from the legislative system of division in some provinces are —

- property held in joint title;
- property acquired after separation;
- property covered in a marriage agreement;
- the proceeds of an insurance policy other than insurance in respect of property, unless the proceeds are compensation for a loss to both spouses;
- a gift or inheritance from a third person;
- damages or a right to damages for personal injury, nervous shock, mental distress, loss of guidance, care, and companionship; or the part of a settlement that represents those damages; and
- business property to which the other spouse made no direct or indirect contribution.

2.2 The matrimonial home

The matrimonial home (that is, the home within which the couple lives during the course of the marriage) receives slightly different treatment. The right of possession is separate from the right of ownership. The home cannot be sold or mortgaged without the signature of the other spouse or a court order, even if the title to the house is in the name of one spouse only. Provincial family legislation also provides that both spouses have an equal right to reside in the home after separation and until divorce or the final settlement of the property issues between the spouses. The court can therefore make an order that one spouse has exclusive right to occupy the family home for whatever period of time the court finds appropriate along with the right to use the household goods, and that order can be registered on the title to the property. By putting the right of occupancy on the title, the property cannot be sold without the purchaser's awareness of the problem. The court can also order that the spouse to whom the court has awarded the right to exclusive occupancy be put on the lease as the tenant in place of the non-occupying spouse.

3. Property for Non-Married Couples

As discussed above, common-law or same-sex partners must carefully consider the manner in which they want their property to be owned in the relationship. Cohabitation agreements are not used very often; but without one, a common-law couple who decide to separate can find the process much harder, because there is no presumption of equal ownership. The law takes the stance that everything that was brought into the relationship is the exclusive property of the individual who brought it in, unless it can be shown that the other person made a direct financial contribution or an indirect contribution, such as doing all the housework, childcare, or repair work, thereby making it possible for the other spouse to run a business or in some way earn more money or acquire goods or property of any kind.

If property is registered in the name of one spouse only but the other makes contributions to the purchase or maintenance of the property, the law of trusts will apply. This law allows a presumption to be made that the owning spouse was holding part of the property in trust for the other spouse. The size of the portion is determined by evaluating the amount and nature of the direct and indirect contribution. Any discussions or understandings about the roles and responsibilities of each will be part of the determination process.

Clearly, financial records should be kept of all household transactions and purchases, or a cohabitation agreement should be created. A cohabitation agreement is especially important if one spouse has less property and less financial ability but is willing to make substantial indirect contributions to the running of the household and the maintenance of the property. Same-sex couples may wish to review Sample 2: Cohabitation Agreement for Same-Sex Couples.

3.1 Trust law

Often, the less well-off spouse tries to compensate by doing most of the household chores, shopping, and cooking. That spouse may even do all the organizing of repairs. As mentioned above, the law of trusts comes into this situation. After evaluating the evidence of the direct and indirect contributions made by the less well-off spouse, a court could find that some portion of the property (or business) owned by the other spouse was held in trust for the non-owning spouse. As a result, that spouse would be entitled to be compensated for his or her contributions. However, the application of the law of trusts usually requires that the less well-off spouse start a court case to overcome the presumption of ownership and must prove in detail the direct and indirect contributions he or she made to entitle him or her to a share in the property. That spouse may end up with nothing or with very little, although the courts are now more willing to find entitlement than they were in the past. There should be a considerable amount at stake to make it worthwhile, not only in terms of legal fees but also in terms of the stress of bringing domestic affairs under the scrutiny of the legal system. For this reason, it's wise to have a cohabitation agreement in place before the relationship breaks down.

Example

If Linda owned the condo into which Jacqui moved and the title remained in Linda's name alone, Jacqui would be entitled to recover the exact amount she contributed to the mortgage payments. In addition, she could recover something for the fact that she painted the entire interior of the condo herself and bought the paint with her own money. Each contribution of that type — considered an indirect contribution, because it is not a direct payment to the mortgage — would have to be quantified. Linda would then have to pay Jacqui that amount upon separation.

3.2 Gifts

There are also instances in which the non-purchasing spouse may acquire property as a result of being gifted the property by the owning spouse.

An example of gifting would be if, say, Linda had said to Jacqui, "When you move in with me, you become half-owner of the condo." Jacqui would have a good argument that Linda had gifted half of the condo to her. There would, however, have to be substantial corroborating evidence of that statement, preferably in writing, for Jacqui to be able to prove that she was entitled to half the value of the condo as a result of being gifted it by Linda. In most cases, if it is, in fact, the intention of one partner to give the other half of such property, that partner would put the other's name on the title as joint owner.

3.3 Joint ownership

Registering property in the names of both spouses as joint owners means that each owner has the right to deal fully with the entire property as if it were his or her own, except in the case of sale, when both signatures would be required. Jointly owned property is automatically divided 50-50 upon sale. If one person dies, the survivor becomes the sole owner without the property becoming part of the deceased's estate. Joint ownership is the simplest way for non-married spouses to hold property equally. There may still be a dispute about the right to share equally by application of the law of trusts, but such a dispute will be an uphill battle, given the clear evidence of an intention to share equally.

4. Children

Many provinces explicitly legislate that custody and access cannot be dictated by a cohabitation or marriage agreement (though support obligations can be included) on the assumption that custody and access follow biology or may be otherwise best determined by court order. Nonetheless, the variety of parenting arrangements in place these days makes it useful to consider drafting a cohabitation agreement to include terms regarding these issues. An agreement can be written that concerns only child care, custody, and support. (Such an agreement is usually referred to as a custody agreement, or, in nonlegal language, a parenting agreement.) The agreement can be structured to cover issues while the spouses are cohabiting as well as to determine how parenting will be handled in the event of separation (except in the provinces in which cohabitation agreements can't deal with custody; see Chapter 1, section **3.**).

Agreements with respect to children are particularly useful for people who are bringing children into a relationship or for cases in which a child is conceived through non-traditional means. In those situations, an agreement can be especially helpful in defining the role of the non-biological parent. Even in those provinces in which custody may not be handled by agreement, terms can be drawn up regarding the education and moral training of the child.

An agreement can bind only the people who are parties to it; that is, it is binding only on those people who sign the document. This fact must be kept in mind by anyone drafting a parenting agreement that makes reference to a biological parent who is not a party to the agreement (for instance, an ex-spouse). For example, say Jack and Joseph want to make an agreement that states that Jack's son, Mark, will always be welcome at Jack and Joseph's recreational property. They cannot bind Jack's ex-wife to any agreement regarding this access. When and how often Mark gets to visit Jack would be binding on Jack's ex-wife only as part of a separation agreement between the two of them or a court order to which they are both parties. All that Jack and Joseph's agreement can say is that Joseph cannot deny Mark the right to come to the recreational property co-owned by Jack and Joseph.

Another aspect of agreements regarding children is that the superior court of the province in which the child is principally resident will always have the right to interfere with the agreement (if application is made to the court). Even in those provinces that do not restrict terms regarding children in a cohabitation agreement, the superior court has a power called *parens patriae*. That is, common law gives superior court judges a residual and overriding power to make orders regarding children, regardless of what the parents might have decided and regardless of legislation.

The court has to consider and apply the rule known as "the best interests of the child." For example, if the agreement between Jack and Joseph states that Mark can use the recreational property as described above, Mark's mother could, if she felt she had reason, apply to the court to ask the court to order that Mark not be allowed access to Jack and Joseph's recreational property. The court would hear evidence on whether or not such an order would be in Mark's best interest and could make an order contrary to the terms of the agreement between Jack and Joseph, despite the fact that Mark's mother was not a party to the agreement.

Terms regarding child support can also always be changed by the court. For example, a couple may set out in an agreement that one of them is obligated to pay the child's school expenses, while the other pays for the clothing. But if they made that agreement when the child was four years old, the spouse responsible for the school expenses might object if the other spouse later thinks that they should send the child to a private school; but the other spouse may believe that the agreement has set out a binding arrangement. However, the court could be asked to interfere on the basis that the change to private school was a change of circumstances not contemplated by the parties at the time they made the agreement. In other words, it is difficult to make an agreement provide for changes over a long period of time. Also, the parties cannot agree to prevent the court from interfering in matters of financial obligations in the nature of child support (or, for that matter, spousal support, which is discussed below).

5. Spousal Support

While formerly only married couples had the legal obligation to support each other whether they were living together or not, now provincial legislation requires common-law and same-sex partners to support each other if they have been living together for a statutorily set length of time (one to five years, depending on the province). Recent judicial decisions are making it clear that it is difficult, although not impossible, for married couples to contract out of this obligation. There is little reason for the courts to make different decisions for non-married couples.

If couples want to be financially independent of each other, they can and should explicitly state so in a cohabitation agreement, along with laying out a framework for how they will manage household expenses. Such a clause is necessary to show that the intended financial separation is maintained, even though the spouses are sharing accommodation. The issue of spousal support comes up only when the parties are separated. Spouses who have maintained financial independence throughout the relationship may want to continue this independence after separation.

If the parties wish to deal with support in the event of one of them dying, they would be best off doing so through the terms of a will. From the point of view of drafting a legally binding cohabitation agreement, it is very difficult to predict the future. How long will the relationship last? How old will each of the spouses be at the time of separation? What will be the state of their health? Will they have had children? Will both continue working full-time? It is very difficult to draft terms that take all these factors into consideration. The answers to these questions will determine whether or not the agreement as drafted can stand at the time of separation.

For these reasons, it is generally better to let the question of spousal support be answered by the provincial legislation and the court's interpretation of the application of the law to the particular situation.

4
Specific Considerations

Sometimes a couple will want to make specific provisions in a domestic contract to cover real estate or a business owned by one or the other of them. In addition, a couple may want to draft terms dealing with the disposition of property on the death of a spouse. This chapter examines these situations, as well as the problem of enforcement of the terms of a contract.

1. Real Estate

Most often, the real estate a couple owns is the home in which they live and perhaps a recreational property. The home may be a single-family dwelling, a condominium property (or, depending on the term used in the provincial legislation, a strata-title property), or a manufactured home. It may be owned by one or both of the spouses or it may be rented.

Before deciding on the terms of a cohabitation agreement, both spouses should be aware of their rights to the property under the law of the province in which they reside and in which the property is found. In Ontario, for example, the Family Law Act states that a married couple cannot contract out of the legislation that states that both spouses have a right of occupancy even though only one of them might be on title. However, a non-married couple can.

If you are drafting an agreement with the intention of dealing with the family home and other sizeable assets, you would be very well advised to consult a lawyer. (You can go to a lawyer solely for the purpose of being advised about the law without any further obligation; or you may find pamphlets and booklets on particular areas of family law at the courthouse or public library in your community.) The treatment of property in family law is very complex (as you might have gathered from Chapter 3). If property is divided in a manner that disadvantages one spouse, and that spouse does not receive compensation for the unequal division in some way that is specified in the agreement, the disadvantaged spouse can ask a judge to review the agreement even if it is many years after the agreement was signed.

In addition, you should ensure that both you and your spouse understand the value of the property and are aware of any encumbrances on title. Encumbrances are usually the mortgage(s) and may also include things such as rights of way for hydro or for a public access path. It is important that you both know the details of who owns the encumbrance (for instance, does the bank hold the mortgage?), as well as how long the encumbrance is to be on title and how much it is worth. If one spouse was made a joint owner, was he or she aware the property was mortgaged and of what obligations came with joint ownership?

It is particularly important that you and your spouse fully discuss any mortgages. If the property is to go into the name of one of the spouses upon separation, will that spouse be able to have his or her name on the mortgage alone? Can the mortgage be paid off in full without penalty? These are questions that must be asked of the bank holding the mortgage.

Related to those questions, of course, is the question of whether or not the spouse who is getting the house will be able to afford not only the mortgage but also the upkeep of the house. Remember that title to property can be transferred, but the obligation of the person in whose name the property is mortgaged continues. That is, the bank will still have the right to go after the person whose name is on the mortgage separately from the person on title to the house.

A common feature of cohabitation agreements is an option whereby one spouse may purchase the other spouse's interest in the jointly held property if they separate. In discussing the terms of such an option, consider when the option to purchase comes into being: will this happen on the date of separation or one month later? How long does the person wishing to purchase the other's interest have to exercise the option — three months? Six months? How is the purchase price determined (e.g., independent appraisal)? What are the terms for payment of the purchase price (monthly installments for ten years)? If the property is to be sold on separation, consider the mechanics of how the sale will be handled and by whom.

Bear in mind, too, that though property is held in joint title during cohabitation or marriage, a cohabitation agreement may still provide for an unequal division upon separation. The agreement can provide that the property be sold and the proceeds be divided on a percentage basis. As long as the term is fair in the particular circumstances of the relationship, the division will be upheld. "Fair in the circumstances" will depend on such things as the length of the relationship and whether or not one spouse was staying at home and raising the children. The longer the relationship lasts and the more one spouse's income was reduced by the having of and/or caring for children, the closer to equal the percentages should be, unless there are clearly stated and understandable reasons for the inequality or some form of compensation for the inequality (for example, spousal support).

2. Provisions on the Death of One Spouse

A marriage agreement does not replace a will, although the agreement can make provisions that take effect on the death of one of the spouses. A will is not a contract between two people; it is a statement of one person's wishes. It is wise for each party to an agreement to make a will at the same time as the agreement is written. The will should be consistent with the terms of the agreement and should cover the same ground as is covered by the agreement. A will can make more provisions than the agreement does, but the agreement cannot provide for more than is in the will.

For example, the agreement can specify that each spouse is to make a will naming the other spouse as his or her beneficiary. Alternatively, for agreements in which the spouses are retaining sole title to their separate property, the agreement can state that each spouse gives up any right to the other's estate upon death and provide for the property to go that spouse's children.

The agreement can go further and state that each spouse promises not to pursue a claim against the estate under provincial law, despite the fact that the legislation gives the surviving spouse (including, in many jurisdictions, common-law and same-sex partners) the right to claim a percentage of the deceased spouse's estate, even if the surviving spouse has not been named in the will or in cases in which the deceased spouse did not have a will. Similarly, a claim to survivor's benefits under a pension plan or annuity scheme can be renounced in a cohabitation agreement.

Any of these types of clauses should be drafted only with the help of a lawyer because of the seriousness of the long-term consequences. Courts can often be persuaded to look at the fairness of an agreement that appears one-sided. For this reason, a spouse who is agreeing to give up a substantial share in property should be given compensation stated clearly in the agreement or the agreement should explicitly state why the agreement is fair as drafted.

3. Provisions When a Business Is Involved

If either or both spouses own shares in a business or intend to own and operate a business while they are cohabitating, a cohabitation agreement is especially important. If a couple is contemplating such an agreement, they must gather information about the company with respect to rules for the holding and transferring of shares. The spouses must decide whether or not the shares and/or the business should be family assets, whether or not the non-owning spouse is going to have a right to the shares in certain circumstances, and what will be done with the shares and/or business upon death or separation. Spouses must take the same considerations into account if one or both are involved in a business run as a partnership, and must be certain to review the partnership agreement before drafting a cohabitation agreement.

It is most important that the spouses review the actual articles and memorandum or by-laws (depending on the provincial law for corporate structure), and reference these in their cohabitation agreement. The corporate documentation will include clauses on how shares are held, how they can be transferred, and whether there are prohibitions or rules about selling the shares. There may be a separate shareholders' agreement. (If the business is held as a partnership, reference must be made to the partnership agreement.) Both spouses must read documentation on shareholding before they can determine what terms are appropriate for their cohabitation agreement. Finally, the spouses may, in fact, have to consult with the company lawyer or accountant and the other shareholders or partners regarding the provisions they are considering. The company rules may not allow for any transfer of shares to a spouse.

If the spouses intend to operate a family business, rules should be established for, on the one hand, borrowing or otherwise incurring debt; and for, on the other, making capital investments. There should also be some provision in the agreement for taking on new shareholders or partners in the future, and terms should be included regarding transferring shares to people other than the spouses. Obviously, in the event of the spouses separating, plans must be made to deal with the division of family assets. Must the company be liquidated, or will each spouse agree to a mandatory sale or an option to purchase the selling spouse's shares?

If the marriage agreement gives one spouse the option to buy the other's interest upon breakdown, guidelines similar to those set out in Sample 1: Cohabitation/Prenuptial/Marriage Agreement (see Sample section of this book) for sale of the property should be included. Each spouse should pay particular attention to the method of valuation and to income-tax consequences. Each must also bear in mind that sales-tax consequences may attend a sale of assets. If there are other shareholders or partners, their rights must be taken into account, and the spouses will also have to consider the statutory rules and the rights of creditors. Owing to the complexity of these issues, spouses in this situation should consult both a lawyer and an accountant.

What follows here are three examples of domestic situations complicated by business considerations. None of these situations is such that the parties can write a cohabitation agreement by themselves. Because of the complexity of the law and the potentially serious financial consequences for each of the spouses, they really must at least consult a lawyer, if not hire one to draft their agreements for them.

Protecting a business vehicle

Maryan and Tony want to draw up a simple agreement that Maryan's business vehicle is not a family vehicle. Maryan does network marketing and bought a vehicle for that purpose. She works from home, and the car does end up being used for some household chores. Tony has an old pickup that he bought before they started living together common law. He likes to take Maryan's newer, more comfortable car when they go out together; however, Tony understands that Maryan bought it with her own earnings for her business.

Maryan wants to ensure that the ownership of the vehicle and its primarily business purpose is protected. Because laws relating to the division or equalization of marital property do not yet apply to common-law couples in most provinces, if Tony wished to gain any share of the vehicle in the event of a separation, he would have to make an argument in court regarding his entitlement to it. He would have to show either that Maryan gifted it to him, which clearly she hasn't, or that he contributed to the cost of purchasing or running the vehicle, which, in fact, is not so. For common-law couples, use alone is not sufficient to establish a claim to property that is legally owned by one spouse. There must be a direct or indirect contribution to that property by the other spouse. (In this case, for example, Tony may have paid for all the repairs — which would be a direct contribution — or have done them himself.) If such a contribution can be shown, that contribution would have to be quantified and the asset divided according to the amount of the contribution.

Protecting stock and pension

Peter and Michel have been living together for several years. During that time, Michel has gradually worked his way into a managerial position at his place of employment. He has acquired a substantial number of shares in the company and may, in the near future, acquire a controlling interest. He has signed a buy-sell agreement with the company that requires him to sell the shares back to the company should he leave its employ. He and Peter have discussed the complexities of the buy-sell agreement and have decided that Peter should not have any right to Michel's shares in the company or its profits. Peter has a good job himself and is always worried that Michel's company is taking too many risks. Peter feels that since Michel is the one bearing the risks, Michel should have the benefits.

They want an agreement that makes it clear that any property or rights to property accumulated during the relationship (including Peter's pension) is exclusively the property of the party who legally owns the property. And as a corollary to that, any debts acquired by each of them are to remain exclusively the obligation of the party who incurred the debt. They agree that upon separation, neither of them has the right to make any claims against the property of the other.

They do have joint title to their home and they are both named on the mortgage. In addition, for the running of the house and for the acquisition of household goods, they have joint chequing and joint savings accounts. They understand that anything they hold jointly will be divided equally on separation, but they want to set out clearly in their agreement that neither will claim that he made a greater contribution than the other, either directly or indirectly, to the running of the house and therefore has a right to share in the other's vehicle or any other asset that the other bought in his own name.

However they do understand that if one of them is economically disadvantaged at the time they separate, the other has an obligation to support him, at least until he is on his feet again. Peter and Michel do love and care for each other. So notwithstanding their desire to keep some of their affairs separate, each is willing to help the other. Their cohabitation agreement will therefore be silent on the issue of support. (However, if they live in one of the provinces in which the right to spousal support has not been extended to same-sex relationships, they must set out under what circumstances spousal support would be owing between them and the method of calculation.)

Protecting a business

Joshua and Ruth have lived together for a year. They are worried about family law being extended to cover common-law relationships, and have decided a cohabitation agreement is necessary in their situation.

Joshua has owned and run a plumbing business for many years. He has been thinking of putting Ruth on the books for tax reasons, but he doesn't want her to have a right to half the business in the event that they separate. If he incorporates his business and gives Ruth shares, he believes that she might, under family law, have a greater or additional entitlement to the business. He is probably right. Any increase in the value of the business from the time they began living together to the time they separate could be included in the valuation of the net worth of the family property, which is especially likely if Ruth's contribution to the home would be considered as having enabled Joshua to keep more money in the business and thus increase its profitability. To avoid this situation, Joshua wants a cohabitation agreement that clearly states that any increase in the value of the business is his alone, save and except for the amount to which Ruth would be entitled as a shareholder.

Ruth understands that by agreeing to those terms, she is decreasing the amount of property in which she would share if the relationship breaks down. She has therefore asked Joshua to transfer title of the house from himself to the two of them as joint owners. That way there can be no question that they are equally entitled to the house. Since it was Joshua's house before they began living together, she feels that she would likely be the one who would have to move, were they to separate. She would then have all the expense of moving and setting up a separate household.

She also believes that Joshua's income and the profit from his business is considerably greater than her income as an office administrator. Thinking about her future, she wants the agreement to include a statement that each understands that he or she has an obligation to support the other, at least for a couple of years following the separation.

Ruth feels that in this way, she will be compensated for her contributions to the household, but she is likely entitled to some level of support regardless of the agreement. She would be better to negotiate a specific entitlement to some other substantial asset, such as Joshua's RRSP, in return for giving up her right to a share in the business.

4. Enforcement

Cohabitation agreements are contracts, as discussed in Chapter 2. Some provinces (British Columbia, Manitoba, Ontario, Nova Scotia, Prince Edward Island, and Newfoundland) have brought them under the governance of provincial family legislation, in the same way marriage agreements are, to make them easier to enforce.

For this reason, couples who enter into cohabitation agreements hoping to avoid the application of provincial family law to their situation may find the court applying that law to their agreement nonetheless. The agreement would be brought before the court as a result of one of the spouses taking an action against the other for the enforcement, interpretation, or voiding of some or all the terms. If you don't live in one of the provinces listed above, you may sue the defaulting spouse using the laws of contract and trust. (See also the explanation at the beginning of Chapter 3).

However, a trip to court may be avoided if your agreement sets out terms providing for the use of an arbitrator or mediator should there be a problem in applying the agreement's terms. (See Sample 1: Cohabitation/Prenuptial/Marriage Agreement for terms calling for the use of an arbitrator.) An arbitrator is trained to listen to the parties, review the documentary evidence, then make a decision — just as a judge would do after a trial. A mediator, though, will work with the parties to help them arrive at their own decision for solving their problems. (See Sample 2: Cohabitation Agreement for Same-Sex Couples regarding terms for the use of a mediator.) Either of these options is cheaper than taking legal action, which may result in a court trial: if the matters in dispute are worth more than the limit of Small Claims Court, you will have to take the matter to your province's superior court and incur lawyer's fees.

If you are going to proceed with a lawsuit regarding the interpretation of a legal agreement, it is really necessary that you consult a lawyer. There is a great deal of case law surrounding cohabitation agreements, and the judge in your case will be applying it to your situation. Without a lawyer, you will be unable to determine what evidence will be most helpful to you to present and what points you should be arguing. The judge cannot advise you and, in fact, cannot use any evidence or law not put forward by the parties involved.

Going to court to enforce an agreement is a very expensive proposition, so mediation or arbitration is a much better alternative. If those alternatives fail, you should consult a lawyer. The advantage of having a lawyer is that he or she will follow up to ensure that the other party does what he or she has undertaken to do. Having a lawyer follow up tends to be effective, and a lawyer can be hired specifically for that purpose.

5 Negotiation

Obviously, before drafting a cohabitation agreement, the spouses must have come to some accord about its contents. Such an accord is reached through negotiation, which *The Canadian Oxford Dictionary* defines as to "confer with others in order to reach a compromise or agreement"; and, alternatively, as to "arrange or settle (a matter) or bring about (a result) by negotiating."

Beginning negotiations is crucial to arriving at an agreement. There are two or three common scenarios that can occur after a couple has decided to create a written cohabitation agreement. Going to see a lawyer and having the lawyer take charge of the negotiations and the drafting of the agreement often works, but again only if both parties are willing to put their signatures on a written document. A mediator may also be helpful in arriving at an agreement if the parties are fearful of what might be stirred up during negotiations or are each reluctant to approach the other without the aid of a disinterested third party.

Often, one spouse will decide that a written cohabitation agreement is the way to settle property issues, issues concerning children, or spousal roles. That spouse will go ahead and draft a contract without discussing the content with the other spouse, and then will simply hand his or her spouse the document and ask him or her to sign it. At that point, useful negotiations might begin, but often both parties see the written document as the initiating spouse's unshakeable position: why else would that person have gone to all the trouble of creating the written document? The two spouses may end up having a reasonable discussion about the issues raised in the document, but another document is seldom drafted because of the unpleasantness caused by the first one.

Another common scenario is that both spouses agree to create a written agreement and begin discussing its content, but never end their discussions or never arrive at a point at which they want to write things down. One of them may be distrustful and not knowledgeable about his or her legal rights. Alternatively, by virtue of discussing their property and long-term plans, they feel that they understand and trust each other, so an agreement is no longer seen to be necessary.

1. Decide Why a Cohabitation Agreement Is Desirable

The first step, then, in arriving at an agreement that can be put into written contract form is for *both* spouses to sit down and agree to negotiate a written agreement. The first matter for the spouses to discuss is why one or the other spouse has suggested a cohabitation agreement be created. Usually, there is a specific reason for negotiating an agreement. For example, there might be a large inheritance in the offing. Or one spouse might not want to repeat the mistakes of his or her last relationship, and as a result, wants a cohabitation agreement that will be effective if separation becomes necessary. One spouse might own a business and want to keep it separate from the family property, or shareholders in the spouse's business might want the new spouse to agree in writing that there are limits to his or her potential entitlement to a share of the business. The spouses might want the document to be part of their plans for dealing with their estates upon death. An agreement between the spouses on why an agreement is necessary is clearly essential.

2. Disclosure and Valuation

Once both spouses understand why an agreement should be drafted, they should decide on a strategy or game plan for working out the details. Keeping in mind that full disclosure is an essential element in a valid and binding agreement, the spouses should prepare documentation on their assets and liabilities, including an indication of the ownership and value of all their debts and property, including cash,

RRSPS, pensions, and securities. Any life, medical, or disability insurance policies would be included in the disclosure, as well as the nature and size of any inheritances expected. If there are children from previous relationships, information about the financial commitments, written agreements, or court orders in place between the biological parents must be put on the table. If one spouse holds shares in a private company, the by-laws and share agreement (particularly the buy-sell terms) for that company are an essential component of the disclosure.

If the proposed agreement is meant to deal only with something very specific, such as ownership of the matrimonial home or the family business, the range of information the spouses must disclose can be limited, but care should be taken that everything that is in fact relevant is disclosed. It is quite surprising how many people are unwilling to reveal the details of their finances, property holdings, or third-party affairs (e.g., biological parents, business) to their new spouses. But without detailed disclosure, a valid and binding cohabitation agreement cannot be assured.

3. Topics to Be Covered

Once the information is on the table, the couple can set out the topics they must discuss to arrive at an agreement. (See Checklist 1.) A good way to proceed from that point, especially if there are more than one or two areas to be covered, is for each spouse to set out either orally or in writing their needs and wishes with regard to each topic. Again, the question of why the topic should be in the agreement must be considered. Is it to avoid the provincial family legislation? Is it to protect particular property? Is it to make provision for special terms of support in the event of separation? Is it to supplement a shareholders' agreement? It is also important to consider whether the terms should be fixed for all time or whether there should be provision for change or even termination of the agreement at a certain point in the future.

The parties must understand that emotions are a factor in the process. Negotiations are generally helped by making room for each spouse to talk about his or her feelings and expectations before making proposals for actual terms. In this way, the importance of each topic to each spouse can be clarified, as can each spouse's willingness

CHECKLIST 1
COHABITATION/MARRIAGE AGREEMENT

Have you included —

- ❏ the agreement date, that is, the date signed by the last person to sign?
- ❏ the full legal names and addresses of both spouses?
- ❏ a statement of purpose of agreement (i.e., to enter into a formal and binding agreement in anticipation of marriage or cohabitation and for mutal love and affection)?
- ❏ the date on which the marriage or cohabitation will start or did start?
- ❏ the full legal names, birthdates, and parentage of any children involved?
- ❏ a statement of items, specifically described, to be dealt with in the agreement (i.e., ownership of property, household financial arrangements, responsibility for children, disposition of property upon separation, support of spouses or children upon separation)?
- ❏ a statement identifying the schedules of property attached to agreement?
- ❏ a detailed statement by each party of his or her income, assets, and liabilities; that disclosure has been complete; and that each has reviewed the other's statement and is familiar with income, assets, and liabilities of the other?
- ❏ a clause regarding support arrangements between you and your spouse during cohabitation or a clause stating that each spouse is self-supporting? (If one spouse agrees to support the other, you must include the details regarding of what this support will consist.)
- ❏ a clause regarding spousal support arrangements in the event of separation? (Once again, if you and your spouse agree to maintenance in the event of separation, you must detail the exact nature of the maintenance.) To ensure currency, this clause will need to be reviewed each time the spouses' circumstances change.
- ❏ a clause regarding support of children? (If included, detail the exact nature of the support, and when and under what conditions such support may terminate.)
- ❏ a clause regarding provision for custody and guardianship of children in the event of separation? (Detail the exact nature of these provisions. Be aware, also, that clauses regarding custody and guardianship of children are not

CHECKLIST 1 — CONTINUED

enforceable by law in most provinces [see Chapter 3, section **4.**] although they can be considered an expression of your wishes.) A statement regarding the wishes of the parents for the moral and educational training of the children can be included.

- ❑ clauses regarding ownership of property? (Detail whether property brought into the relationship will remain separate or will become jointly owned and registered on title. Detail also how property acquired by each spouse during the relationship will be owned.)
- ❑ a clause (or clauses) regarding the marital home (i.e., owned by one spouse or both; proportion of ownership in the event of separation; responsibility for mortgage, repairs, and maintenance)?
- ❑ a clause (or clauses) regarding the ownership and disposition of any other real estate upon separation?
- ❑ a clause regarding domestic arrangements (i.e., division of household chores [note that such a clause is not enforceable in court])?
- ❑ a clause dealing with ownership of and responsibility for pets?
- ❑ a clause regarding vehicles (i.e., ownership, registration, use, and responsibility for payments, repairs, maintenance, and insurance)?
- ❑ a clause (or clauses) dealing with the ownership and disposition of gifts to one spouse or the other?
- ❑ a clause dealing with the ownership and disposition of inheritances?
- ❑ a clause (or clauses) dealing with the ownership of savings, securities, insurance benefits, RRSPs, and pension plans?
- ❑ a clause dealing with responsibility for payments of any existing debts and debts incurred in future?
- ❑ a clause setting out how disputes will be resolved (i.e., by mediation or arbitration)?
- ❑ acknowledgement by both parties of independent legal advice or that they have willingly and in full knowledge of their legal right to such advice opted to dispense with such advice?

— or lack thereof — to be flexible on each topic. The spouses are also able to identify their commonalities and differences on each topic prior to negotiating wording, and can reach agreement on some terms before going on to deal with those on which they appear to differ. If, at the end of these preliminaries, the spouses appear to be far apart, it might be wise for them to consider consulting a mediator or lawyer.

4. Drafting Tips

Below are some drafting tips you may wish to review before writing your own domestic contract. Sample 1: Cohabitation/Prenuptial/Marriage Agreement, which follows this chapter, illustrates the tips and the paragraph letters and numbers given in the tips refer to the agreement, so you may wish to refer to it as you read through this section.

- *Use recitals of undisputed facts:* Beginning the first section of the agreement with "Whereas" is simply a way of proclaiming the beginning. Alternatively, you could use the heading "Undisputed Facts." Some agreements have no formal beginning other than the letters identifying the paragraphs. The "recitals" are a series of statements agreed to by both parties as basic facts.
- *Use definitions:* Paragraphs B and L of the Sample 1 could be considered definitions; that is, the paragraphs make it clear what is meant by certain terms (e.g., "parties" or "marriage agreement").
- *Use schedules:* A schedule is a document attached to and incorporated into the agreement by being referenced in the text, as it is here in paragraphs E and F, and more specifically in paragraphs 2 and 3. A schedule is used to provide details that would take up too much space if set out in the body of the agreement.
- *Use complete and proper descriptions:* Paragraph 10 gives the municipal address and the legal description of the property so that there can be no dispute as to which property is being discussed and anyone wanting to do a legal search of the property will be able to do so easily. Similar care should be taken in identifying children: always give their birth dates, along with all their names and parentage as set out in paragraphs C and

D. Pensions, mutual funds, and any financial instrument should all be carefully identified, and their locations should be specified. It is also important to give a complete description of what is included or meant when describing a piece of property. Does the car include the bicycle rack? Does the sailboat include the dingy?

- *Aim for clarity:* Leave no uncertainty as to what is meant. Ambiguity can make a clause void and unenforceable.
- *Avoid repetition.*
- *Be correct:* When identifying ownership and monetary values, refer to the original documentation to ensure accuracy. It may be years before you have any need to consult your agreement. The details must be accurate to prevent confusion and misinterpretation.
- *Tie up loose ends:* In the sample agreement, paragraphs 13(d), 22, 30, and 32 are examples of the parties attempting to deal with a variety of situations that may arise. If the agreement is to be effective over a period of several years, all possible future considerations must be addressed at the time of drafting.
- *Avoid agreements to agree:* Paragraph 30 could be considered an agreement to agree on future major expenses, but a conflict may nonetheless develop. Later in the agreement, at paragraph 47, under the heading Conflict Resolution, there is a provision for settling disputes, but this would be an expensive solution. It would be better to put into paragraph 30 some guidelines for when agreement between the parties on an expense would be appropriate (for example, repair of a leaky roof). Despite this clause, however, the parties are, in fact, engaged in a mutual enterprise called living together in the same house. This common purpose usually reflects an agreement to agree.
- *Be practical:* The buy/sell provisions in paragraphs 18 to 26 are an example of the kind of practical detail that makes an agreement effective and useful. Without the detail, an agreement remains an expression of ideas but does not provide concrete solutions to potential problems. The parties also have to be able to fulfil the terms. For example, paragraph 13(c) gives a percentage of the mortgage that is affordable for the spouse in question.

- *Know the law:* It is important to be familiar with the law so you can draft terms that will help you and your spouse avoid having the legislation applied to your situation, should that be what you desire. In the case of paragraph 44, for example, most provincial family law now obligates common-law spouses to support each other upon separation if there is financial need. Paragraph 44 may not be sufficient to allow you to avoid that law if you and your spouse separate many, many years after signing the agreement and your circumstances have changed significantly. For example, if one of you is in financial need due to prolonged illness or unemployment, the party concerned may have a valid case for support, as this situation was unforeseen at the time of the agreement. With regard to paragraph 52, you have to understand trust law as it applies to property law for non-married couples, as set out earlier in this book. When dealing with the transfer of property, you will want to be aware of tax consequences (e.g., income tax, property transfer tax, provincial sales tax, and GST).
- *Avoid legalese:* The first sentence of paragraph 49 uses the words "partnership, agency, or joint tenancy" in their legal sense. The second sentence gives the basic meaning and would be clear and legally sufficient without the first sentence. Similarly, in paragraph 50 the words "heirs, executors, administrators, and assigns" are legal terms but are generally understood, with the possible exception of "assigns." (Assigns are those who gain an interest in property by legal transfer of title or by gaining legal interest in the property.) With regard to paragraph 52, you may want to read the section on trust law for non-married couples in Chapter 3.
- *Use precedents with caution:* The samples in this book are examples of "precedents"; that is, they are a standard form of the agreement, given only to show what may go into an agreement. However, not all paragraphs will be appropriate for each reader's circumstances. You must study each term and come to your own conclusion about which terms can be used as written, which terms need to be altered, and which terms need to be created for your particular situation.

Part Two
SAMPLES

SAMPLE 1
COHABITATION/MARRIAGE AGREEMENT

COHABITATION/PRENUPTIAL/MARRIAGE AGREEMENT

THIS AGREEMENT made in triplicate this 8th day of April 20 0-

BETWEEN:

Jack Sole

(referred to as "Jack Sole")

AND:

Jill Single

(referred to as "Jill Single")

WHEREAS:

A. Jack Sole and Jill Single ~~reside~~/will reside together in a committed relationship.

B. Jack Sole and Jill Single (referred to simply as the "Parties") ~~began~~/will begin to live together on or about May 1, 200-.

C. ______ has ______ children of a prior marriage, ~~namely~~,

______, born ______,

______, born ______,

______, born ______,

______, born ______,

OR

Jack Sole has no children.

D. ______ has ______ children of a prior marriage, ~~namely~~,

______, born ______,

______, born ______,

______, born ______,

______, born ______,

OR

Jill Single has no children.

J.S. J.S.

SELF-COUNSEL PRESS — CDN-CC (1-1) 03

SAMPLE 1 — CONTINUED

E. Jack Sole has the assets and liabilities outlined in the attached Schedule A and no others.

F. Jill Single has the assets and liabilities outlined in the attached Schedule B and no others.

G. Any undisclosed assets owned by either party shall be deemed to be a joint asset subject to equal division.

H. The parties are both self-supporting.

I. (i) ______________________ is solely responsible for any support payable ~~for~~ his children, ______________________, ______________________, ______________________, ______________________,

(ii) ______________________ is solely responsible for any support payable ~~for~~ her children, ______________________, ______________________, ______________________, ______________________,

J. The Parties are entering into this Agreement —

(a) to resolve all issues that may arise as to ownership and management of property, real or personal, communal or otherwise, owned, or which may be owned by either of them at a later time, jointly or severally;

(b) to determine management of, ownership in, and division of assets during their cohabitation;

(c) to determine responsibilities regarding children;

(d) to determine management of, ownership in, and division of assets; and

(e) to determine support of the children and each other in the event of separation or termination of their relationship.

K. The Parties intend this Agreement to be the final settlement and release of their respective claims and interests relating to the property set out in this Agreement and the attached Schedules, and to claims to maintenance and support.

L. This Agreement is intended to be both a marriage agreement and a cohabitation agreement between the Parties.

IN CONSIDERATION of the promises and mutual covenants contained herein, the Parties agree as follows:

J.S. J.S.

SELF-COUNSEL PRESS — CDN-CC (1-2) 03

INTENT OF AGREEMENT

1. Jack Sole and Jill Single separately acknowledge that:

(a) their relationship resembles marriage;

OR

~~(a) their relationship is/will be marriage;~~

(b) in the course of the relationship, each of them will confer benefits upon the other;

(c) benefits conferred by one upon the other are gifts, and the making of these gifts does not result in an unjust enrichment of the recipient to the detriment of the donor;

[From among paragraphs (d), (e), (f), and (g), choose those that apply to your situation. Strike through those that do not apply to your situation.]

(Separate property) (d) neither Party intends to share legal or beneficial ownership of her or his separate property, owned before or acquired after the making of this Agreement, save and except where set out in this Agreement or where the Parties expressly agree in writing; and

(Separate Property) (e) neither Party shall rely upon the oral expression, or conduct that may suggest the expression, of an intention by one Party to hold property or a portion of property in trust for the other Party.

(Equal shares) (f) ~~both Parties intend to share equally the legal and beneficial ownership of their separate property, owned before or acquired after the making of this Agreement, save and except where set out in this agreement or where the Parties expressly agree in writing; and~~

(Equal shares) (g) ~~all property of whatever kind purchased by either or both Parties while cohabitating will be the joint property of both Parties and is held in equal shares with equal right to its use and enjoyment save and except where set out in this Agreement or where the Parties expressly agree in writing.~~

2. Jack Sole states and agrees that all of his/~~her~~ assets and liabilities as of the date of this Agreement will be accurately listed in a schedule which, upon being initialled by both Jack Sole and Jill Single, shall be attached to this Agreement as Schedule A and form part of this Agreement. Jack Sole acknowledges that Jill Single is relying on this statement as to the accuracy of Schedule A.

3. Jill Single states and agrees that all of her/~~his~~ assets and liabilities as of the date of this Agreement will be accurately listed in a schedule which, upon being initialled by both Jill Single and Jack Sole, shall be attached to this Agreement as Schedule B and form part of this Agreement. Jill Single acknowledges that Jack Sole is relying on this statement as to the accuracy of Schedule B.

J.S. J.S.

SELF-COUNSEL PRESS — CDN-CC (1-3) 03

SAMPLE 1 — CONTINUED

4. The Parties each agree that it is his or her intent that, if the parties cohabit, this Agreement shall be a full and final settlement of all property issues arising prior to their cohabitation, during their cohabitation, and on the breakdown of their relationship. The Parties each agree that the terms of this Agreement shall survive any marriage or divorce of the parties, and that the Agreement shall constitute a marriage agreement.

(Separate property)

5. The Parties each agree that it is his or her intent that, subject to this Agreement, __Jack Sole__ shall retain the assets listed in Schedule A and __Jill Single__ shall retain the assets listed in Schedule B as her or his sole property if the Parties separate.

OR

(Equal shares)

~~5. The Parties each agree that it is his or her intent that, subject to this Agreement, the assets referred to in Schedule A and Schedule B shall be divided in equal shares if the Parties separate.~~

INTERPRETATION

6. Unless otherwise specifically defined by this Agreement, the words used in this Agreement shall have the meaning ordinarily applied to such words.

7. If any portion of this Agreement is found to be illegal, unenforceable, void or voidable, each of the remaining paragraphs shall remain in full force and effect as a separate contract.

(Name your province of residence)

(State the name of the high court of your province)

8. This Agreement shall be interpreted and take effect in accordance with the laws of the province/~~territory~~ of __Ontario__, and the Parties agree that any action concerning or relating to this Agreement in any respect shall be brought in the province/~~territory~~ of __Ontario Superior__ Court for this purpose.

9. The section titles in this Agreement are for convenience only and shall not be construed to affect the meanings of the sections so entitled.

PROPERTY

10. __Jack Sole__ is the registered owner of the property and premises located at __123 My Street__, in the City of __My City__, in the Province/~~Territory~~ of __Ontario__, more legally known and described as:______, District Lot______, ~~Strata Plan~~______ (hereinafter called "the Property").

(Insert description as found in property tax notice)

11. __Jack Sole__ is and shall remain the sole registered owner of the Property.

12. __Jack Sole__ purchased the Property on __February 15, 200-__, for __$230,000.00__, and the current fair market value is approximately __$235,000.00__.

J.S. J.S.

SELF-COUNSEL PRESS — CDN-CC (1-4) 03

13. Notwithstanding the above, Jack Sole agrees that while he/~~she~~ and Jill Single cohabit, Jill Single shall acquire an interest in the Property on an incremental basis as follows:

(a) Jack Sole shall have sole title to and ownership of forty PERCENT (40 %) of the Property in recognition of his/~~her~~ Down payment of $ 92,000.00 (the "down payment"), free of any claim by Jill Single, this being the current equity in the Property;

(b) The remaining sixty PERCENT (60 %) interest in and to the Property represents the mortgages against the Property in the amount of $ 138,000.00, the liability for this share of the Property shall be divided equally between Jack Sole and Jill Single;

(c) Jill Single's share of the equity in the Property shall rise as the mortgages are paid down at the rate of 1 and ½ PERCENT (1½ %) per year, PROVIDED HOWEVER that Jill Single shall pay ~~his~~/her share of the mortgage payments;

(d) Jill Single shall have the option to pay to Jack Sole a lump sum payment for the purchase of an additional interest in the Property in proportion to the amount of ~~his~~/her payment, which proportion and additional interest shall be agreed in writing between the Parties and added as an addendum to this Agreement.

MORTGAGE

14. There is a mortgage/loan/line of credit in the sum of $138,000.00, in the name of Jack Sole, dated February 15, 200-, registered against the Property and held by Jack Sole, (now referred to in this Agreement simply as the "Mortgage").

15. The monthly payment due and owing pursuant to the Mortgage is currently in the amount of $900.00 per month, including principal and interest and not including property taxes (now referred to in this Agreement simply as the "the Mortgage Payments").

(Equal payments) 16. Jack Sole and Jill Single shall share the Mortgage Payments equally, such that each of the Parties pay $450.00 per month.

OR

(Payments in different amounts) ~~16. The Parties shall share the Mortgage Payments, such that __________ shall pay $________ (__________) and __________ shall pay $________ (__________).~~

17. Each Party hereto shall not further encumber the mortgage or sell his or her interest, whether legal or beneficial, in and to the Property in any way whatsoever.

J.S. J.S.

SAMPLE 1 — CONTINUED

BUY/SELL PROVISIONS

18. If Jack Sole wishes to sell his/~~her~~ interest in and to the Property, he/~~she~~ shall first give written notice of such intention to Jill Single, and she/~~he~~ shall have the first option to purchase the interest of Jack Sole at a price to be determined by a current appraisal of the market value of the property; this option shall remain open for a period of ninety (90) days from the date of the receipt by Jill Single of the written notice.

19. If Jill Single wishes to sell her/~~his~~ interest in the Property, she/~~he~~ shall first give written notice of such intention to Jack Sole, and he/~~she~~ shall have the first option to purchase the interest of Jill Single at a price to be determined by a current appraisal of the market value of the Property; which said option shall remain open for a period of ninety (90) days from the date of the receipt by Jack Sole of the written notice.

20. In the event of the termination of the relationship between Jack Sole and Jill Single, for any reason whatsoever, Jack Sole shall have the first option to purchase the interest of the other at a price to be determined by a current appraisal of the market value of the Property; which said option shall remain open for a period of ninety (90) days from the date of the termination of the relationship.

21. In the event that neither of the Parties wishes to exercise her or his option as set out herein or upon the expiry of the option period, the Parties shall list the Property for sale with a Multiple Listing Service at a listing price to be determined by agreement or as set out in Paragraph 22 herein, BUT UNDER NO CIRCUMSTANCES shall the Property be sold at a price less than the original purchase price, unless otherwise mutually agreed in writing.

22. In the event there is no agreement between the Parties as to the listing price or option purchase price, it shall be set by obtaining THREE (3) independent realtor appraisals and taking an average of the THREE (3) appraisals.

23. The fees and costs of the said appraisals of the Property shall be borne equally between the Parties.

24. An offer from a bona fide purchaser within two PERCENT (2%) of the listing price shall be accepted by both Parties unless both Parties mutually agree in writing to decline the offer.

25. In the event that the Property is sold, the proceeds of the sale shall be applied first to the commission to any real estate agency involved in the sale; second, to any outstanding taxes; third, to any legal or other costs involved in the sale; fourth, to the payment of the Mortgage; fifth, to the payment to Jack Sole of his/~~her~~ forty PERCENT (40%) share of the Property; sixth, to any defaults as may be outstanding to the non-defaulting Party, as set out in Paragraph 31 herein.

26. The balance of the sale proceeds shall be divided equally between Jack Sole and Jill Single.

J.S. J.S.

SELF-COUNSEL PRESS — CDN-CC (1-6) 03

USAGE OF THE PROPERTY

27. Jack Sole and Jill Single shall share equally in the use and occupation of the Property.

UTILITIES, TAXES, GENERAL MAINTENANCE, AND LIVING EXPENSES

(Equal payments) 28. Jack Sole and Jill Single shall share equally in the following expenses and costs:

(a) property taxes;
(b) strata fees;
(c) hydro, cable, and telephone;
(d) house insurance;
(e) groceries; and
(f) capital expenses, such as repairs and extra strata expenses.

OR

(Different payments) 28. Each Party shall be responsible only for those payments listed below beside which his or her initials appear:

property taxes	______	house insurance	______
strata fees	______	groceries	______
hydro, cable, and telephone	______	capital expenses, such as repairs and extra strata expenses	______

(Equal payments) 29. The Parties shall share equally the cost of all utilities, and non-capital repairs as necessary for the general upkeep of the Property and fixtures therein and each shall pay ONE-HALF (1/2) of such costs as and when they become due and owing.

OR

(Payments in different amounts) 29. The Parties shall share in the cost of all utilities and non-capital repairs as necessary for the general upkeep of the Property and fixtures therein as follows: ____________________ shall pay______% and____________________ shall pay______% of such costs as and when they become due and owing.

30. The Parties agree that no major expense, including renovation, repair, and redecoration, shall be incurred, unless otherwise mutually agreed; save and except in the case of an emergency when immediate steps must be taken to ensure the safety of the Property.

DEFAULTS

31. In the event that either Party shall fail to pay any or all of his or her payments as set out in this Agreement, such default shall be covered by the other Party, and all monies, costs, and obligations outstanding, together with interest at the prevailing bank lending interest rate accrued thereon, shall be deducted from the share in the net sale proceeds of the defaulting Party and the sum so deducted shall be used to reimburse the other Party for her or his outlay and expenses in respect of the default.

J.S. J.S.

SELF-COUNSEL PRESS — CDN-CC (1-7) 03

SAMPLE 1 — CONTINUED

32. In the event that the share in the net sale proceeds of the defaulting Party as set out herein is not sufficient to satisfy the outstanding amount owing, together with accrued interest, he or she shall continue to be responsible for such default and shall be held liable to indemnify and save the other Party harmless from all costs, outlays, actions, and claims arising from the said default.

33. All defaults in payments and costs shall accrue interest at the prevailing bank lending interest rate at the time of the default until such payments and costs are paid in full.

OTHER PROPERTY, ASSETS, AND LIABILITIES

(Separate property)

34. EXCEPT AS SPECIFICALLY PROVIDED HEREIN, property brought into the relationship by each of the Parties, and specifically those major assets set out in Schedule A and Schedule B hereto or purchased solely by one Party during the relationship, shall remain the sole property of such Party, and Jack Sole and Jill Single hereby agree that they shall remain separate as to personal and real property with respect to all interest in personal and real property of either as the same existed prior to their relationship.

OR

(Equal shares)

34. EXCEPT AS SPECIFICALLY PROVIDED HEREIN, property brought into the relationship by each of the Parties, including those major assets set out in Schedule A and Schedule B hereto or purchased solely by one Party during the relationship shall be the joint property of both Parties, held in equal share. However, any and all property inherited by either Party from that Party's family shall remain that Party's separate property, with no right or entitlement to that property to the non-inheriting spouse.

(Separate liability)

35. Liabilities incurred by each of the Parties shall remain the personal liability of such Party.

OR

(Joint liability)

35. Liabilities incurred by either Party during the period of cohabitation are the joint obligation and responsibility of both Parties. If either Party wishes to contract for a debt of more than $__________.________, the other Party must be told in advance and must give his/her consent in writing for that specific obligation before it is incurred.

36. Property and assets acquired jointly by the Parties shall be shared equally between the Parties as joint tenants.

37. In the event of the termination of the relationship, for whatever reason, Jack Sole and Jill Single agree to divide such joint property and joint assets in an equitable and amicable manner. Should such amicable division not be possible or practicable, the Parties agree to submit the decision respecting the division of such joint property and assets to arbitration in accordance with Paragraph 47 hereof.

CHILDREN

38. It is the intention of both Parties not to conceive a child within three (3) years from the date of this agreement.

J.S. J.S.

SELF-COUNSEL PRESS — CDN-CC (1-8) 03

39. The Parties agree not to have more than ___two___ (___2___) children in this relationship.

40. The children born in this relationship will have the surname ___Sole–Single___.

41. The children born to_______________ in any previous relationship ~~will continue to be the sole responsibility of_______________ unless custody changes to_______________~~, in which case the next paragraph will apply to those children equally.

42. (a) The Parties agree that they will each be jointly and equally responsible for the financial, physical, and emotional upbringing, care, and support of their children. As much as possible, the Parties will each put in equal time, energy, and resources to the emotional, mental, and physical well-being of their children.

(b) If at any point it is not possible for the Parties each to make an equal contribution, the Parties will negotiate and agree on the terms and length of time for the unequal contribution.

(No religion) 43. The Parties acknowledge that they are not followers of any religion or religious organization. If for any reason either of the Parties wishes the children to participate in any religion, the other must agree. If no agreement can be reached, then there will be no participation in any religion by the children.

OR

(Religion specified) 43. The Parties acknowledge that they are followers of the_______________ religion, and it is the intention of both ~~Parties that their~~ children participate in the_______________ ~~religion.~~

SUPPORT AND MAINTENANCE

(Self-supporting) 44. ___Jack Sole___ and ___Jill Single___ hereby agree that they are each able to support and maintain themselves and neither Party shall take action for support and maintenance for themselves now, in the future, or in the event of the termination of the relationship.

OR

(Support obligated) 44. In the event that_______________ and_______________ decide to live separate and apart, neither Party shall be obligated to support the other unless their relationship lasted a minimum of________ (__________) years and:

(a) the earning capacity of one Party is under a serious financial disadvantage because of the obligations placed upon him or her by the relationship; or

(b) one of the Parties is incapable of reasonably supporting himself or herself because of mental or physical infirmity, illness, or the demands of caring for the children of the relationship.

If either of the situations set out in sub-paragraphs (a) or (b) of section 44 exists, then we agree that the non-incapacited Party will pay__________________ PERCENT (_______%) of his or her net yearly income as support to the other Party until the financial disability no longer exists, or for a period of__________ (_____) months/years.

J.S. J.S.

SELF-COUNSEL PRESS — CDN-CC (1-9) 03

(Note that clauses regarding custody and access may not be enforceable in some provinces.)

45. (a) In the event that Jack Sole and Jill Single decide to live separate and apart and there are dependant children of the relationship, the children will be in the joint custody of both Parties, with their primary residence from the date of separation being with Jill Single. The Parties will be reasonable in ensuring that Jack Sole has frequent and regular visits with the children.

(b) If there are dependant children of the relationship at the time of separation, then Jill Single will continue to live in the family home. Jack Sole and Jill Single will be responsible for those payments listed below beside which their initials appear:

mortgage payments	Jack S.	house insurance	Jill S.
property taxes	Jill S.	groceries	Jill S.
~~strata fees~~		capital expenses, such as repairs and extra strata expenses	Jack S.
hydro, cable, and telephone	Jill S.		

(c) If there are dependent children of the relationship at the time of separation, then Jack Sole shall pay child support in accordance with the Child Support Guidelines, and to that end Jack Sole shall provide a copy of his/~~her~~ tax return and income tax assessment annually to Jill Single no later than June 15 each year, until the youngest child ceases to be dependant or attains the age of 21. Child support will be paid by Jack Sole by providing Jill Single with 12 postdated cheques in the appropriate Guideline table amount, starting the month following the provision to Jill Single of the annual income tax return and assessment.

CANADA PENSION AND OTHER BENEFITS

(No division of pensions)

46. In the event of the termination of the relationship, for whatever reason, the Parties hereto agree that neither Party shall make application for a division of the other Party's unadjusted pensionable earnings pursuant to the Canada Pension Plan Act, R.S.C. 1985, C. C-8 and amendments and regulations thereto, nor for a division of the other Party's pension plan or pension schemes through employment, and each Party shall indemnify and save harmless the other Party from any such division.

OR

(Pensions may be divided)

~~46. In the event of the termination of the relationship, for whatever reason, save and except for the death of either Party, whereupon it is contemplated that the survivor may apply for any or all benefits on the event of death, the Parties hereto agree to equally divide their unadjusted pensionable earnings pursuant to the Canada Pension Plan Act, R.S.C. 1970, C. C-5 and amendments and regulations thereto, as well as their pension plans or pension schemes through employment.~~

J.S. J.S.

SELF-COUNSEL PRESS — CDN-CC (1-10) 03

CONFLICT RESOLUTION

47. All matters in difference in relation to this Agreement shall be referred to the arbitration of a single arbitrator, if the Parties agree upon ONE (1), otherwise to THREE (3) arbitrators, one to be appointed by each Party and a third to be chosen by the first two named before they enter upon the business of arbitration. The award and determination of such arbitrator or arbitrators, or any TWO (2) of such THREE (3) arbitrators, shall be binding upon the Parties and their respective heirs, executors, administrators, and assigns.

48. The request for arbitration may be made by either Party and shall be in writing and delivered to the other Party.

GENERAL CLAUSES

49. This Agreement is not intended to create a partnership, agency, or joint tenancy. This Agreement does not give any Party the authority or power to act for or undertake any obligations or responsibilities on behalf of the other Party, unless otherwise agreed in writing.

50. This Agreement shall continue to the benefit of and be binding upon the heirs, executors, administrators, and assigns of each of the Parties in the event of the death of either of them.

51. Neither Party shall, without the previous consent in writing of the other Party, assign his or her interest in any jointly acquired property or any part thereof or otherwise encumber his or her interest in and to the jointly acquired property by gift, donation, transfer, or otherwise.

RELEASES

52. The Parties release each other from any claims they may have against each other's separate property by way of a declaration of trust, resulting, constructive or otherwise, other than any claims arising under or to enforce the provisions of this Agreement.

53. The Parties agree to be governed by the terms of this Agreement, and neither Party shall commence an action against the other Party pursuant to any provincial or federal legislation as may be applicable to force a sale of the Property, and each Party shall indemnify and save the other Party harmless from any such actions, claims, and costs thereof.

LEGAL ADVICE, DISCLOSURE, FAIRNESS

54. Each Party acknowledges that she or he has had independent legal advice or has freely waived the right to such independent legal advice; understands her and his respective rights and obligations under this Agreement; is signing this Agreement voluntarily, without fraud, duress, or undue influence; and has affirmed her or his belief that the provisions of this Agreement are adequate to discharge the present and future responsibilities of the Parties and that this contract will not result in circumstances that are unconscionable or unfair to any Party.

AMENDMENTS AND UNDERTAKINGS

55. The Parties may amend any of the terms in this Agreement by a writing signed by them and witnessed and endorsed on this Agreement or attached, and all such amendments shall be followed and have the same force and effect as if they had originally been in and formed part of this Agreement.

I.S. J.S.

SAMPLE 1 — CONTINUED

56. Jack Sole and Jill Single shall at all times and upon reasonable request put their signature to all such documents and give all such further assurances and do all such acts required for the purpose of giving effect to the terms, agreements, and provisions contained in this Agreement.

57. This Agreement shall remain in force and effect until the Parties agree in writing to terminate this Agreement.

IN WITNESS WHEREOF Jack Sole has hereunto set his/~~her~~ hand and seal at the City of My City, in the Province/~~Territory~~ of Ontario, on the 8th day of April, 200-.

SIGNED, SEALED AND DELIVERED)
by Jack Sole)
in the presence of:)

I.M. Certified) I.M. Certified
Name
1414 Your Street)
My City, Ontario)
Address
Teacher)
Occupation

IN WITNESS WHEREOF Jill Single has hereunto set ~~his~~/her hand and seal at the City of My City, in the Province/~~Territory~~ of Ontario, on the 8th day of April, 200-.

SIGNED, SEALED AND DELIVERED)
by Jill Single)
in the presence of:)

I.C. Ewe) I.C. Ewe
Name
1367 New Street)
My City, Ontario)
Address
Sales Manager)
Occupation

J.S. J.S.

SELF-COUNSEL PRESS — CDN-CC (1-12) 03

SCHEDULE A

Major Assets and Property owned by Jack Sole *as his sole property:*

Assets		Value
1.	Property	$235,000.00
2.	Toyota Tercel 1990	$2,000.00
3.	Credit Union RRSP #xxxxxxxx	$40,000.00
4.	Credit Union #xxxxxx	
	Mutual Fund	$9,500.00
5.	U-Do-It Group Investments	
	Dividend Fund #xxxxxxx	$6,200.00
	Japanese Fund #xxxxxxx	$1,800.00
	Money Market Fund #xxxxxx	$600.00
	European Growth Fund (new)	$500.00
6.	I-Do-It Group #xxxxxx	
	Dividend Fund	$4,000.00
	($2000 belongs to___________, rest is split equally)	
7.	Household items	
	Furniture, Stereo, TV, and Kitchen items	$25,000.00

Debts and liabilities

1.	Mortgage on the Property	$138,000.00
2.	Bank of Your City	
	Personal line of credit	$5,500.00
3.	Visa credit card	$1,179.00

J.S. J.S.

SELF-COUNSEL PRESS — CDN-CC (1-13) 03

SAMPLE 1 — CONTINUED

SCHEDULE B

Major Assets and Property owned by Jill Single *as her sole property:*

Assets	Value
1. Furniture Dresser, Radio, Antiques	$7,000
2. VW Jetta 1994	$11,000.00
3. Investing Now Group #xxxxxx Dividend Fund	$2,000.00
4. RRSP #xxxxxx	$67,780.00

Debts and liabilities

1. Bank of Montreal Personal line of credit	$3,500.00
2. Lease Loan, VW Jetta	$7,500.00
3. MasterCard credit card	$667.00

J.S. J.S.

SELF-COUNSEL PRESS — CDN-CC (1-14) 03

SAMPLE 2
COHABITATION AGREEMENT FOR SAME-SEX COUPLES

COHABITATION AGREEMENT FOR SAME-SEX COUPLES

THIS AGREEMENT made in triplicate this 7th day of July 20 0-

BETWEEN:

John Right

(hereinafter called "John Right")

OF THE FIRST PART

AND:

Mike Left

(hereinafter called "Mike Left")

OF THE SECOND PART

WHEREAS:

A. John Right and Mike Left reside together in a committed relationship.

B. John Right and Mike Left (the "Parties") commenced residing together on or about May 1, 200-;

C. ________ has ____ children of a prior relationship, ~~namely~~,

________, ~~born~~ ________,

________, born ________,

________, born ________,

OR

C. John Right has no children.

~~D. ________ was divorced/separated from the father/mother of his/her children on ________, ________.~~

E. ________ has ____ children of a prior relationship, ~~namely~~,

________, born ________,

________, born ________,

________, born ________,

OR

E. Mike Left has no children.

J.R. M.L.

SELF-COUNSEL PRESS — CDN-CC (2-1) 03

SAMPLE 2 — CONTINUED

~~F. ______________________________ was divorced/separated from the father/mother of his/her children on __________________________, _________.~~

G. John Right has the assets and liabilities outlined in Schedule A hereto and no others.

H. Mike Left has the assets and liabilities outlined in Schedule B hereto and no others.

I. Any undisclosed assets owned by either party shall be deemed to be a joint asset subject to equal division.

J. The parties are both self-supporting.

~~K. ______________________________ is solely responsible for the support of his/her children, namely,~~

~~______________________________,~~

~~______________________________,~~

~~______________________________,~~

~~and receives/does not receive child support from the father/mother of the children.~~

~~L. ______________________________ is solely responsible for the support of his/her children, namely,~~

~~______________________________,~~

~~______________________________,~~

~~______________________________,~~

~~and receives/does not receive child support from the father/mother of the children.~~

M. The Parties are entering into this Agreement —

(a) to resolve all issues that may arise as to ownership and management of property, real or personal, communal or otherwise, owned or which may hereafter be owned by either of them, jointly or severally;

(b) to determine management of, ownership in, and division of assets during their cohabitation;

(c) to determine management of, ownership in, and division of assets; and

(d) to determine support of ~~the children and~~ each other in the event of separation or termination of their relationship.

N. The Parties intend this Agreement to be the final settlement and release of their respective claims and interests relating to the property set out in this Agreement and claims to maintenance and support.

IN CONSIDERATION of the promises and mutual covenants contained herein, the Parties agree as follows:

J.R. M.L.

SELF-COUNSEL PRESS — CDN-CC (2-2) 03

1. INTENT OF AGREEMENT

1.1 John Right and Mike Left separately acknowledge that:

(a) their relationship is tantamount to spousal;

(b) in the course of the relationship, each of them will confer benefits upon the other; benefits conferred by one Party upon the other are gifts, and the making of these gifts does not result in an unjust enrichment of the recipient to the detriment of the donor;

[From among paragraphs (c), (d), (e), and (f), choose those that apply to your situation. Strike through those that do not apply to your situation.]

(Separate property) (c) neither Party intends to share legal or beneficial ownership of his/~~her~~ separate property, owned before or acquired after the making of this Agreement, save and except where set out in this Agreement or where the Parties expressly agree in writing; and

(Separate Property) (d) neither Party shall rely upon the oral expression, or conduct which may suggest the expression, of an intention by one Party to hold property or a portion of property in trust for the other Party.

(Equal shares) (e) both Parties intend to equally share the legal and beneficial ownership of their separate property, owned before or acquired after the making of this Agreement, save and except where set out in this agreement or where the Parties expressly agree in writing; and

(Equal shares) (f) all property of whatever kind purchased by either or both Parties while cohabitating will be the joint property of both Parties and is held in equal shares with equal right to its use and enjoyment save and except where set out in this Agreement or where the Parties expressly agree in writing.

1.2 John Right represents and agrees that all of his/~~her~~ assets and liabilities as of the date of this Agreement will be accurately listed in a schedule which, upon being initialled by both John Right and Mike Left, shall be attached hereto as Schedule A and form part of this Agreement. John Right acknowledges that Mike Left is relying on this representation as to the accuracy of Schedule A.

1.3 Mike Left represents and agrees that all of his/~~her~~ assets and liabilities as of the date of this Agreement will be accurately listed in a schedule which, upon being initialled by both Mike Left and John Right, shall be attached hereto as Schedule B and form part of this Agreement. Mike Left acknowledges that John Right is relying on this representation as to the accuracy of Schedule B.

J.R. M.L.

SELF-COUNSEL PRESS — CDN-CC (2-3) 03

SAMPLE 2 — CONTINUED

1.4 The Parties each agree that it is their intent that, if the Parties cohabit, this Agreement shall be a full and final settlement of all property issues arising prior to their cohabitation, during their cohabitation, and on the breakdown of their relationship. The Parties each agree that the terms of this Agreement shall survive any separation of the parties.

(Separate property)

1.5 The Parties each agree that it is their intent that, subject only to this Agreement, John Right shall retain the assets listed in Schedule A, and Mike Left shall retain the assets listed in Schedule B as his/~~her~~ sole property hereto in the event of separation and termination of the relationship of the Parties.

OR

(Equal shares)

1.5. The Parties each agree that it is his or her intent that, ~~subject to this Agreement, the assets referred to in Schedule A and Schedule B shall be divided in equal shares if the Parties separate.~~

2. INTERPRETATION

2.1 Unless otherwise specifically provided herein, the words used in this Agreement shall have the meaning ordinarily applied to such words.

2.2 If any portion of this Agreement is found to be illegal, unenforceable, void, or voidable, each of the remaining items shall remain in full force and effect as a separate contract.

(Name your province of residence)

(State the name of the high court of your province)

2.3 This Agreement shall be interpreted and take effect in accordance with the laws of Ontario, and the Parties agree that any action concerning or relating to this Agreement in any respect shall be brought in Ontario and that each agrees to the jurisdiction of the Ontario Superior Court for this purpose.

2.4 The section titles in this Agreement are for convenience only and shall not be construed to affect the meanings of the sections so entitled.

3. PROPERTY

(Insert legal description as found in property tax notice)

3.1 John Right is the registered owner of the property and premises located at 129 My Street, in the City of My City, in the Province of Ontario, more legally known and described as:_______________ ______________________________(hereinafter called "the Property") which is the home of John Right.

3.2 John Right is and shall remain the sole registered owner of the Property.

~~*[Clauses 3.3 to 3.4 to be used if one Party is to acquire an interest in the Property owned by the other party.]*~~

~~3.3 ____________________ purchased the Property on ____________________, for____________________, and the current fair market value is approximately____________________.~~

J.R. M.L.

SELF-COUNSEL PRESS — CDN-CC (2-4) 03

3.4 Notwithstanding the above,________________________ agrees that while he/she and _______________________ cohabit,______________________ shall acquire an interest in the Property on an incremental basis as follows:

(a) ________________________________ shall have sole title to and ownership of ______________ PERCENT (_______%) of the Property in recognition of his/her down payment of $_______________________ (the "down payment"), free of any claim by_______________________, this being the current equity in the Property;

(b) The remaining______________ PERCENT (__________%) interest in and to the Property represents the mortgages against the Property in the amount of $_____________________________, the liability for this share of the Property shall be divided equally between_________________________ and_____________________;

(c) ________________________'s share of the equity in the Property shall rise as the mortgages are paid down at the rate of_____ and_____ PERCENT (_________%) per year, PROVIDED HOWEVER that________________ shall pay his/her share of the mortgage payments;

(d) _______________________ shall have the option to pay to___________________ a lump sum payment for the purchase of an additional interest in the Property in proportion to the amount of his/her payment, which proportion and additional interest shall be agreed in writing between the Parties and added as an addendum to this Agreement.

4. MORTGAGE

4.1 There is a mortgage/loan/line of credit in the sum of $170,000.00, in the name of John Right, dated November 30, 200-, registered against the Property and held by My Bank, (now referred to in this Agreement simply as the "Mortgage").

4.2 The monthly payment due and owing pursuant to the Mortgage is currently in the amount of $1,000.00 per month, including principal and interest and not including property taxes (now referred to in this Agreement simply as the "the Mortgage Payments").

(Equal payments) ~~4.3 ________________________ and___________________________ shall share the Mortgage Payments equally, such that each of the Parties pay________________________________ per month.~~

OR

(Payments in different amounts) 4.3 The Parties shall share the Mortgage Payments, such that John Right shall pay $600.00 (six hundred dollars) and Mike Left shall pay $400.00 (four hundred dollars).

~~4.4 Each Party hereto shall not further encumber the mortgage or transfer his/her interest, whether legal or beneficial, in and to the Property in any way whatsoever.~~

J.R. M.L.

SELF-COUNSEL PRESS — CDN-CC (2-5) 03

5. BUY/SELL PROVISIONS

[Clauses 5.1 to 5.9 to be used if both parties have an interest in the Property.]

5.1 If__________________ wishes to sell his/her interest in and to the Property, he/she shall first give written notice of such intention to__________________________, and she/he shall have the first option to purchase the interest of_________________________________ at a price to be determined by a current appraisal of the market value of the property; this option shall remain open for a period of____________ (______) days from the date of the receipt by_______________ ______________________________of the written notice.

5.2 If___________________ wishes to sell her/his interest in the Property, she/he shall first give written notice of such intention to___________________________ and he/she shall have the first option to purchase the interest of______________________ at a price to be determined by a current appraisal of the market value of the Property; which said option shall remain open for a period of______________ (_________) days from the date of the receipt by_________________ of the written notice.

5.3 In the event of the termination of the relationship between_________________________ and_________________________, for any reason whatsoever,_________________________ shall have the first option to purchase the interest of the other Party at a price to be determined by a current appraisal of the market value of the Property; which said option shall remain open for a period of______________ (________) days from the date of the termination of the relationship.

5.4 In the event that neither of the Parties wishes to exercise his/her option as set out herein or upon the expiry of the option period, the Parties shall list the Property for sale with a Multiple Listing Service at a listing price to be determined by agreement or as set out in Paragraph 5.5 herein, BUT UNDER NO CIRCUMSTANCES shall the Property be sold at a price less than the original purchase price, unless otherwise mutually agreed in writing.

5.5 In the event there is no agreement between the Parties as to the listing price or option purchase price, it shall be set by obtaining THREE (3) independent realtor appraisals and taking an average of the THREE (3) appraisals.

5.6 The fees and costs of the said appraisals of the Property shall be borne equally between the Parties.

5.7 An offer from a bona fide purchaser within__________ PERCENT (_________%) of the listing price shall be accepted by both Parties unless both Parties mutually agree in writing to decline the offer.

5.8 In the event that the Property is sold, the proceeds of the sale shall be applied first to the commission to any real estate agency involved in the sale; second, to any outstanding taxes; third, to any legal or other costs involved in the sale; fourth, to the payment of the Mortgage; fifth, to the payment to________________________ of his/her______________ PERCENT (_______%) share of the Property; sixth, to any defaults as may be outstanding to the non-defaulting Party, as set out in Paragraph 7.1 herein.

I.R. M.L.

SELF-COUNSEL PRESS — CDN-CC (2-6) 03

5.9 The balance of the sale proceeds shall be divided ~~equally between ____________ and ____________~~.

6. USAGE OF THE PROPERTY

6.1 John Right and Mike Left shall share equally in the use and occupation of the Property during the course of their relationship.

(Equal payments)

~~6.2 ____________ and ____________ shall share equally in the following expenses and costs:~~

~~(a) property taxes;~~
~~(b) strata fees;~~
~~(c) hydro, cable, and telephone;~~
~~(d) house insurance;~~
~~(e) groceries; and~~
~~(f) capital expenses, such as repairs and extra strata expenses.~~

OR

(Different payments)

6.2 Each Party shall be responsible only for those payments listed below beside which his/~~her~~ initials appear:

property taxes	JR	house insurance	JR
~~strata fees~~		groceries	ML
hydro, cable, and telephone	ML	capital expenses, such as repairs and extra strata expenses	JR

(Equal payments)

~~6.3 The Parties shall share equally the cost of all utilities, and non-capital repairs as necessary for the general upkeep of the Property and fixtures therein and each shall pay ONE-HALF (1/2) of such costs as and when they become due and owing.~~

OR

(Payments in different amounts)

6.3 The Parties shall share in the cost of all utilities and non-capital repairs as necessary for the general upkeep of the Property and fixtures therein as follows: John Right shall pay 60 % and Mike Left shall pay 40 % of such costs as and when they become due and owing.

6.4 The Parties agree that no major expense, including renovation, repair, and redecoration, shall be incurred, unless otherwise mutually agreed; save and except in the case of an emergency when immediate steps must be taken to ensure the safety of the Property.

[Clause 6.5 to be used if one Party retains ownership of the Property.]

6.5 John Right as owner of the property, shall be solely responsible for any and all capital repairs, improvements, and replacements with respect to the Property and the appliances therein.

J.R. M.L.

SELF-COUNSEL PRESS — CDN-CC (2-7) 03

7. DEFAULTS

[To be used if one Party retains ownership of the Property.]

7.1 In the event that either Party shall fail to pay any or all of his/~~her~~ payments as set out in this Agreement, such default shall be covered by the other Party, and all monies, costs, and obligations outstanding together with interest at the prevailing bank lending interest rate accrued thereon shall be deducted or added, as the case may be, to the Settlement Payout to __Mike Left__ as set out herein.

OR

[To be used if both Parties have an interest in Property.]

~~7.1 In the event that either Party shall fail to pay any or all of his or her payments as set out in this Agreement, such default shall be covered by the other Party, and all monies, costs, and obligations outstanding, together with interest at the prevailing bank lending interest rate accrued thereon, shall be deducted from the share in the net sale proceeds of the defaulting Party and the sum so deducted shall be used to reimburse the other Party for her or his outlay and expenses in respect of the default.~~

8. OTHER PROPERTY, ASSETS, AND LIABILITIES

(Separate property) 8.1 Property brought into the relationship by each of the Parties and specifically those assets set out in Schedules A and B hereto or purchased solely by one Party during the relationship shall remain the sole property of such party, and __John Right__ and __Mike Left__ hereby agree that they shall remain separate as to personal and real property with respect to all interest in personal and real property of either as the same existed prior to their relationship.

OR

(Equal shares) ~~8.1 EXCEPT AS SPECIFICALLY PROVIDED HEREIN, property brought into the relationship by each of the Parties, including those major assets set out in Schedule A and Schedule B hereto or purchased solely by one Party during the relationship shall be the joint property of both Parties, held in equal share. However, any and all property inherited by either Party from that Party's family shall remain that Party's separate property, with no right or entitlement to that property to the non-inheriting Party.~~

(Separate liability) 8.2 Liabilities incurred by each of the Parties shall remain the personal liability of such Party.

OR

(Joint liability) ~~8.2 Liabilities incurred by either Party during the period of cohabitation are the joint obligation and responsibility of both Parties. If either Party wishes to contract for a debt of more than $__________.________, the other Party must be told in advance and must give his/her consent in writing for that specific obligation before it is incurred.~~

8.3 Property and assets acquired jointly by the Parties shall be shared equally between the Parties as joint tenants.

J.R. M.L.

SELF-COUNSEL PRESS — CDN-CC (2-8) 03

8.4 In the event of the termination of the relationship, for whatever reason, John Right and Mike Left agree to divide such joint property and joint assets in an equitable and amicable manner. Should such amicable division not be possible or practicable, the Parties agree to submit the decision respecting the division of such joint property and assets to mediation in accordance with Clause 12 hereof.

9. CANADA PENSION OR OTHER PENSION BENEFITS

(No division of pensions)

9.1 In the event of the termination of the relationship, for whatever reason, save and except for the death of either Party, whereupon it is contemplated that the survivor may apply for any or all benefits on the event of death, the Parties hereto agree that neither Party shall make application for a division of the other Party's unadjusted pensionable earnings pursuant to the Canada Pension Plan Act, R.S.C. 1970, C. C-5 and amendments and regulations thereto, nor for a division of the other Party's pension plan or pension schemes through employment, and each Party shall indemnify and save harmless the other Party from any such division.

OR

(Pensions to be divided)

9.1 In the event of the termination of the relationship, for whatever reason, save and except for the death of either Party, whereupon it is contemplated that the survivor may apply for any or all benefits on the event of death, the Parties hereto agree to equally divide their unadjusted pensionable earnings pursuant to the Canada Pension Plan Act, R.S.C. 1970, C. C-5 and amendments and regulations thereto, as well as their pension plans or pension schemes through employment.

10. SUPPORT AND MAINTENANCE

(Self-supporting)

10.1 Both John Right and Mike Left covenant and agree that they each are self-supporting and shall not claim interim or permanent maintenance from each other now or in the future, and forever discharges and releases each other from all such claims pursuant to any law or statute.

OR

(Support obligated)

10.1 In the event of termination of the Parties' relationship, ____________________ agrees to pay support and maintenance to ____________________ of $________ (________) per month for________ months/years, or until____________________.

10.2 ____________________ acknowledges and agrees that he/she and the father/mother of his/her children, namely,

____________________,

____________________,

____________________,

have the sole obligation for the support of his/her children and that, notwithstanding the close relationship between____________________ and the children,____________________ shall not claim interim or permanent child support for the support of the children from ____________________now or in the future.

J.R. M.L.

SELF-COUNSEL PRESS — CDN-CC (2-9) 03

10.3 ______________________ acknowledges and agrees that he/she and the father/mother of his/her children, namely,

______________________,

______________________,

______________________,

have the sole obligation for the support of his/her children and that, notwithstanding the close relationship between ______________________ and the children, ______________________ shall not claim interim or permanent child support for the support of the children from ______________________ now or in the future.

11. SEPARATION

[Clauses 11.1 to 11.5 to be used where one Party retains ownership of the Property.]

11.1 IN THE EVENT of separation and termination of the relationship, for whatever reason, save and except for the death of either of the Parties, Mike Left shall vacate the Property within THIRTY-ONE (31) days of the date agreed between the Parties as the separation date.

11.2 IN THE FURTHER EVENT that the Parties cannot agree on the separation date, Mike Left shall vacate the Property within THIRTY-ONE (31) days of receipt of written notice by John Right to vacate the Property.

11.3 IN THE EVENT of separation and termination of the relationship before July 7, 200-, John Right shall pay to Mike Left in full recognition of any deprivation Mike Left has incurred as a result of his/~~her~~ contributions to the Property ~~and the family~~ and in full and final settlement of any and all claims arising from the relationship of the Parties, the sum of five hundred DOLLARS ($ 500.00) (hereinafter called "the Settlement Payout") forthwith upon him/~~her~~ vacating the Property. Such amount is in lieu of any claim for a share in the property or support or maintenance.

11.4 IN THE EVENT of separation and termination of the relationship after, July 7, 200-, and including July 7, 200-, John Right shall pay to Mike Left in addition to the Settlement Payout, the sum of one thousand dollars ($ 1,000.00) per year for every year the relationship continues after July 7, 200-. Calculations shall be made *pro rata* on any partial year. Such amount is in lieu of any claim for a share in the property or support or maintenance.

11.5 In addition, the total amount of the Settlement Payout shall be increased by a percentage increase based on the percentage increase, if any, in the Canadian Consumer Price Index for the My City, Ontario area from the date of this Agreement to the date of separation. Such amount is in lieu of any claim for a share in the property or support or maintenance.

J.R. M.L.

SELF-COUNSEL PRESS — CDN-CC (2-10) 03

12. CONFLICT RESOLUTION

12.1 If a dispute arises concerning this Agreement, neither of the Parties shall commence court proceedings until the Parties have attempted mediation.

12.2 The Parties shall share equally the costs of mediation.

12.3 The request for mediation may be made by either Party and shall be in writing and delivered to the other Party.

13. GENERAL CLAUSES

13.1 This Agreement is not intended to create a partnership, agency, or joint tenancy. This Agreement does not give any Party the authority or power to act for or undertake any obligations or responsibilities on behalf of the other Party, unless otherwise agreed in writing.

13.2 This Agreement shall continue to the benefit of and be binding upon the heirs, executors, administrators, and assigns of each of the Parties hereto.

13.3 Neither Party shall, without the previous consent in writing of the other Party, assign his/~~her~~ interest in any jointly acquired property or any part thereof or otherwise encumber his/~~her~~ interest in and to the jointly acquired property by gift, donation, transfer, or otherwise.

14. RELEASES

14.1 The Parties hereby release each other from any claims they may have against each other's separate property by way of a declaration of trust, resulting, constructive or otherwise, other than any claims arising under or to enforce the provisions of this Agreement.

15. LEGAL ADVICE, DISCLOSURE, FAIRNESS

15.1 John Right and Mike Left each acknowledge that he/~~she~~ has had independent legal advice or has freely waived the right to such independent legal advice; understands his/~~her~~ respective rights and obligations under this Agreement; is signing this Agreement voluntarily, without fraud, duress, or undue influence; and has affirmed his/~~her~~ belief that the provisions of this Agreement are adequate to discharge the present and future responsibilities of the Parties and that the contract herein will not result in circumstances that are unconscionable or unfair to any Party.

16. AMENDMENTS AND UNDERTAKINGS

16.1 The Parties may amend any of the terms hereof by a writing signed by them and witnessed and endorsed on this Agreement or appended hereto, and all such amendments shall be adhered to and have the same force and effect as if they had originally been embodied in and formed part of this Agreement.

16.2 John Right and Mike Left shall at all times and from time to time hereafter and upon reasonable request execute all such documents and give all such further assurances and do all such acts required for the purpose of giving effect to the covenants, terms, agreements, and provisions contained in this Agreement.

J.R. M.L.

SELF-COUNSEL PRESS — CDN-CC (2-11) 03

SAMPLE 2 — CONTINUED

16.3 This Agreement shall remain in force and effect until the Parties shall agree in writing to terminate this Agreement.

IN WITNESS WHEREOF John Right has hereunto set his/~~her~~ hand and seal at the City of My City, in the Province/~~Territory~~ of Ontario, on the 7th day of July, 200-.

SIGNED, SEALED AND DELIVERED)
by John Right)
in the presence of:)

I.M. Certified) I.M. Certified
Name
1414 Your Street)
My City, Ontario)
Address
Teacher)
Occupation

IN WITNESS WHEREOF Mike Left has hereunto set his/~~her~~ hand and seal at the City of My City, in the Province/~~Territory~~ of Ontario, on the 7th day of July, 200-.

SIGNED, SEALED AND DELIVERED)
by Mike Left)
in the presence of:)

I.C. Ewe) I.C. Ewe
Name
1367 New Street)
My City, Ontario)
Address
Sales Manager)
Occupation

J.R. M.L.

SELF-COUNSEL PRESS — CDN-CC (2-12) 03

SCHEDULE A

Major Assets and Property owned by John Right *as his~~/her sole~~ property:*

Assets	Value
1. House Vancouver, British Columbia Legal Description: Lot XXXX All interests in and to	Estimated at $310,000.00
2. Contents of the home as at the date of cohabitation and all personal possessions as at the date of cohabitation	Estimated at $28,000.00
3. Automobile 1999 Toyota Corolla	Estimated at $16,000.00

Debts and liabilities

1. Mortgage on the Property	$170,000.00
2. Visa credit card	$760.00
3. My Bank Personal line of credit	$2,500.00

J.R. M.L.

SELF-COUNSEL PRESS — CDN-CC (2-13) 03

SAMPLE 2 — CONTINUED

SCHEDULE B

Major Assets and Property owned by Mike Left *as his/~~her sole~~ property:*

Assets	Value
1. Automobile 1994 Honda Accord	Estimated at $4,000.00
2. All personal possessions and chattel in her/his possession as at the date of cohabitation of the Parties	Estimated at $10,000.00

Debts and liabilities

1. Visa credit card	$1,200.00
2. The Bank Personal line of credit	$5,500.00

J.R. M.L.

SELF-COUNSEL PRESS — CDN-CC (2-14) 03

SAMPLE 3
JOINTLY ACQUIRED ASSET AGREEMENT

JOINTLY ACQUIRED ASSET AGREEMENT

BETWEEN: Paul Purchaser
111 Cash Circle, Rain, BC

AND: Vanda Paule
111 Cash Circle, Rain, BC

1. Paul Purchaser (has/~~have~~) entered into an agreement with *(a)* Sales Department Store to purchase a Chesterfield Suite at a cost of $ 3,000.00 .

(a) Seller's name

2. The payments of $ 150.00 per month are to be made by Paul Purchaser & Vanda Paule to *(a)* Sales Department Store on the 15th day of each month for 20 months/~~weeks~~.

(a) Seller's name

3. Each shall make one-half of the payment to *(a)* Sales Department Store on the date or dates such payments are due.

4. Each shall keep a record of all payments made. Such payments are to be made by cheque or money order.

5. If either Paul Purchaser or Vanda Paule fails to make a payment, the other has the right to make the complete payment and to have his or her interest in the suite increased.

6. If Paul Purchaser and Vanda Paule should separate, and both want to purchase the interest of the other in the suite , a fair price, which takes into account any outstanding payments and the contribution of each shall be agreed upon and a coin tossed. The winner of the coin toss shall then have the right to buy the loser's interest.

P.P. V.P.

SELF-COUNSEL PRESS — CDN-CC (3-1) 03

SAMPLE 3 — CONTINUED

7. If no agreement under paragraph 6 can be reached, the chesterfield suite shall be sold.

~~8. Each shall be entitled to that percentage of the net proceeds which corresponds to the percentage of the payment he or she made of the total price.~~

Delete one ~~OR~~

Each shall be entitled to one-half of the net proceeds realized from the sale.

SIGNED, SEALED AND DELIVERED

on the 30th day of June,

20 0- in the City

of Rain

in the Province of British Columbia

in the presence of:

Ima Witness
Witness's signature

Ima Mary Witness
Witness's name

101 Home Street, Rain, BC
Address

Bank manager
Occupation

Paul Purchaser **seal**
Signature

Paul Purchaser
Name

AND

Walter Witness
Witness's signature

Walter Witness
Witness's name

101 Home Street, Rain, BC
Address

Teacher
Occupation

Vanda Paule **seal**
Signature

Vanda Paule
Name

SELF-COUNSEL PRESS — CDN-CC (3-2) 03

SAMPLE 4
SEPARATELY ACQUIRED ASSET AGREEMENT

SEPARATELY ACQUIRED ASSET AGREEMENT

BETWEEN: Tom Ring
111 Matrimony Street, Regina, Saskatchewan

AND: Wanda Ring
111 Matrimony Street, Regina, Saskatchewan

1. Tom Ring has entered into an agreement with *(a)* Big Sellers Ltd. to purchase a stereo system at a cost of $ 1,500.00.

(a) Seller's name

2. The payments of $ 50.00 per month are to be made SOLELY by Tom Ring to Big Sellers Ltd. on the 10th day of each month for 30 months/~~weeks.~~

3. Both Tom Ring and Wanda Ring intend that the stereo system shall be owned as the sole and separate property of Tom Ring.

4. Wanda Ring consents to Tom Ring purchasing said stereo system and to his/~~her~~ assuming sole responsibility for all payments.

T.R. W.R.

SELF-COUNSEL PRESS — CDN-CC (4-1) 03

SAMPLE 4 — CONTINUED

5. Wanda Ring gives up all and any claim to the stereo system and agrees to consider it the sole and separate property of Tom Ring for all purposes.

SIGNED, SEALED AND DELIVERED

on the 30th day of November,

20 0- in the City

of Regina

in the Province of

Saskatchewan

in the presence of:

Ima Witness
Witness's signature

Ima Mary Witness
Witness's name

301 Watch St., Regina
Address

Tom Ring **seal**
Signature

Teacher
Occupation

Tom Ring
Name

AND

Walter Witness
Witness's signature

Walter Witness
Witness's name

301 Watch St., Regina
Address

Wanda Ring **seal**
Signature

Sales manager
Occupation

Wanda Ring
Name

SELF-COUNSEL PRESS — CDN-CC (4-2) 03

Part Three
BLANK CONTRACTS

COHABITATION/PRENUPTIAL/MARRIAGE AGREEMENT

THIS AGREEMENT made in triplicate this_______ day of__________________ 20____

BETWEEN:

____

(referred to as "____________________")

AND:

____

(referred to as "____________________")

WHEREAS:

A. ____________________________ and____________________________ reside/will reside together in a committed relationship.

B. ____________________________ and____________________________ (referred to simply as the "Parties") began/will begin to live together on or about______________________.

C. ____________________________ has_________ children of a prior marriage, namely,

____________________________, born____________________________,

____________________________, born____________________________,

____________________________, born____________________________,

____________________________, born____________________________,

OR

____________________________ has no children.

D. ____________________________ has_________children of a prior marriage, namely,

____________________________, born____________________________,

____________________________, born____________________________,

____________________________, born____________________________,

____________________________, born____________________________,

OR

____________________________ has no children.

__________ __________

E. ______________________________ has the assets and liabilities outlined in the attached Schedule A and no others.

F. ______________________________ has the assets and liabilities outlined in the attached Schedule B and no others.

G. Any undisclosed assets owned by either party shall be deemed to be a joint asset subject to equal division.

H. The parties are both self-supporting.

I. (i) ________________________ is solely responsible for any support payable for his children, ____________________________,
____________________________,
____________________________,
____________________________,

(ii) ________________________ is solely responsible for any support payable for her children, ____________________________,
____________________________,
____________________________,
____________________________,

J. The Parties are entering into this Agreement —

(a) to resolve all issues that may arise as to ownership and management of property, real or personal, communal or otherwise, owned, or which may be owned by either of them at a later time, jointly or severally;

(b) to determine management of, ownership in, and division of assets during their cohabitation;

(c) to determine responsibilities regarding children;

(d) to determine management of, ownership in, and division of assets; and

(e) to determine support of the children and each other in the event of separation or termination of their relationship.

K. The Parties intend this Agreement to be the final settlement and release of their respective claims and interests relating to the property set out in this Agreement and the attached Schedules, and to claims to maintenance and support.

L. This Agreement is intended to be both a marriage agreement and a cohabitation agreement between the Parties.

IN CONSIDERATION of the promises and mutual covenants contained herein, the Parties agree as follows:

__________ __________

INTENT OF AGREEMENT

1. ______________________________ and__________________________ separately acknowledge that:

(a) their relationship resembles marriage;

OR

(a) their relationship is/will be marriage;

(b) in the course of the relationship, each of them will confer benefits upon the other;

(c) benefits conferred by one upon the other are gifts, and the making of these gifts does not result in an unjust enrichment of the recipient to the detriment of the donor;

[From among paragraphs (d), (e), (f), and (g), choose those that apply to your situation. Strike through those that do not apply to your situation.]

(Separate property) (d) neither Party intends to share legal or beneficial ownership of her or his separate property, owned before or acquired after the making of this Agreement, save and except where set out in this Agreement or where the Parties expressly agree in writing; and

(Separate Property) (e) neither Party shall rely upon the oral expression, or conduct that may suggest the expression, of an intention by one Party to hold property or a portion of property in trust for the other Party.

(Equal shares) (f) both Parties intend to share equally the legal and beneficial ownership of their separate property, owned before or acquired after the making of this Agreement, save and except where set out in this agreement or where the Parties expressly agree in writing; and

(Equal shares) (g) all property of whatever kind purchased by either or both Parties while cohabitating will be the joint property of both Parties and is held in equal shares with equal right to its use and enjoyment save and except where set out in this Agreement or where the Parties expressly agree in writing.

2. ____________________________ states and agrees that all of his/her assets and liabilities as of the date of this Agreement will be accurately listed in a schedule which, upon being initialled by both______________________ and_________________________, shall be attached to this Agreement as Schedule A and form part of this Agreement. ________________________ acknowledges that__________________________ is relying on this statement as to the accuracy of Schedule A.

3. _________________________ states and agrees that all of her/his assets and liabilities as of the date of this Agreement will be accurately listed in a schedule which, upon being initialled by both_________________________ and________________________, shall be attached to this Agreement as Schedule B and form part of this Agreement. __________________ acknowledges that_______________________ is relying on this statement as to the accuracy of Schedule B.

___________ ___________

4. The Parties each agree that it is his or her intent that, if the parties cohabit, this Agreement shall be a full and final settlement of all property issues arising prior to their cohabitation, during their cohabitation, and on the breakdown of their relationship. The Parties each agree that the terms of this Agreement shall survive any marriage or divorce of the parties, and that the Agreement shall constitute a marriage agreement.

(Separate property)

5. The Parties each agree that it is his or her intent that, subject to this Agreement, ______________________ shall retain the assets listed in Schedule A and ____________________ shall retain the assets listed in Schedule B as her or his sole property if the Parties separate.

OR

(Equal shares)

5. The Parties each agree that it is his or her intent that, subject to this Agreement, the assets referred to in Schedule A and Schedule B shall be divided in equal shares if the Parties separate.

INTERPRETATION

6. Unless otherwise specifically defined by this Agreement, the words used in this Agreement shall have the meaning ordinarily applied to such words.

7. If any portion of this Agreement is found to be illegal, unenforceable, void or voidable, each of the remaining paragraphs shall remain in full force and effect as a separate contract.

(Name your province of residence)

(State the name of the high court of your province)

8. This Agreement shall be interpreted and take effect in accordance with the laws of the province/territory of_________________________________, and the Parties agree that any action concerning or relating to this Agreement in any respect shall be brought in the province/territory of________________________________ Court for this purpose.

9. The section titles in this Agreement are for convenience only and shall not be construed to affect the meanings of the sections so entitled.

PROPERTY

10. ____________________________ is the registered owner of the property and premises located at__________________________, in the City of___________________________, in the Province/Territory of__________________________________, more legally known and described as:__________________________________, District Lot___________, Strata Plan____________ (hereinafter called “the Property”).

(Insert description as found in property tax notice)

11. ____________________________________is and shall remain the sole registered owner of the Property.

12. ____________________________ purchased the Property on______________________, for______________________________, and the current fair market value is approximately ______________________________.

____________ ____________

13. Notwithstanding the above,___________________________ agrees that while he/she and ________________________ cohabit,________________________ shall acquire an interest in the Property on an incremental basis as follows:

(a) ___________________________________shall have sole title to and ownership of ______________ PERCENT (______%) of the Property in recognition of his/her Down payment of $______________________ (the "down payment"), free of any claim by______________________, this being the current equity in the Property;

(b) The remaining_______________ PERCENT (_________%) interest in and to the Property represents the mortgages against the Property in the amount of $__________________, the liability for this share of the Property shall be divided equally between_______________________ and__________________________;

(c) ________________________’s share of the equity in the Property shall rise as the mortgages are paid down at the rate of_____ and______ PERCENT (_______%) per year, PROVIDED HOWEVER that____________________ shall pay his/her share of the mortgage payments;

(d) ______________________ shall have the option to pay to____________________ a lump sum payment for the purchase of an additional interest in the Property in proportion to the amount of his/her payment, which proportion and additional interest shall be agreed in writing between the Parties and added as an addendum to this Agreement.

MORTGAGE

14. There is a mortgage/loan/line of credit in the sum of__________________________, in the name of___________________________, dated________________________, registered against the Property and held by______________________, (now referred to in this Agreement simply as the “Mortgage”).

15. The monthly payment due and owing pursuant to the Mortgage is currently in the amount of_____________________________ per month, including principal and interest and not including property taxes (now referred to in this Agreement simply as the “the Mortgage Payments”).

(Equal payments)

16. _____________________________ and________________________ shall share the Mortgage Payments equally, such that each of the Parties pay________________________ per month.

OR

(Payments in different amounts)

16. The Parties shall share the Mortgage Payments, such that____________________________ shall pay $____________ (___________________) and_______________________________ shall pay $______________ (____________________).

17. Each Party hereto shall not further encumber the mortgage or sell his or her interest, whether legal or beneficial, in and to the Property in any way whatsoever.

____________ ____________

BUY/SELL PROVISIONS

18. If__________________ wishes to sell his/her interest in and to the Property, he/she shall first give written notice of such intention to________________________, and she/he shall have the first option to purchase the interest of________________________________ at a price to be determined by a current appraisal of the market value of the property; this option shall remain open for a period of__________ (______) days from the date of the receipt by___________ ________________________of the written notice.

19. If__________________ wishes to sell her/his interest in the Property, she/he shall first give written notice of such intention to________________________, and he/she shall have the first option to purchase the interest of_____________________ at a price to be determined by a current appraisal of the market value of the Property; which said option shall remain open for a period of______________ (______) days from the date of the receipt by________________ ________________________of the written notice.

20. In the event of the termination of the relationship between______________________ and_________________________, for any reason whatsoever,____________________ shall have the first option to purchase the interest of the other at a price to be determined by a current appraisal of the market value of the Property; which said option shall remain open for a period of____________ (_______) days from the date of the termination of the relationship.

21. In the event that neither of the Parties wishes to exercise her or his option as set out herein or upon the expiry of the option period, the Parties shall list the Property for sale with a Multiple Listing Service at a listing price to be determined by agreement or as set out in Paragraph 22 herein, BUT UNDER NO CIRCUMSTANCES shall the Property be sold at a price less than the original purchase price, unless otherwise mutually agreed in writing.

22. In the event there is no agreement between the Parties as to the listing price or option purchase price, it shall be set by obtaining THREE (3) independent realtor appraisals and taking an average of the THREE (3) appraisals.

23. The fees and costs of the said appraisals of the Property shall be borne equally between the Parties.

24. An offer from a bona fide purchaser within________ PERCENT (______%) of the listing price shall be accepted by both Parties unless both Parties mutually agree in writing to decline the offer.

25. In the event that the Property is sold, the proceeds of the sale shall be applied first to the commission to any real estate agency involved in the sale; second, to any outstanding taxes; third, to any legal or other costs involved in the sale; fourth, to the payment of the Mortgage; fifth, to the payment to_________________ of his/her_________________ PERCENT (_______%) share of the Property; sixth, to any defaults as may be outstanding to the non-defaulting Party, as set out in Paragraph 31 herein.

26. The balance of the sale proceeds shall be divided equally between_________________ and____________________________.

__________ __________

USAGE OF THE PROPERTY

27. ________________________ and________________ shall share equally in the use and occupation of the Property.

UTILITIES, TAXES, GENERAL MAINTENANCE, AND LIVING EXPENSES

(Equal payments)

28. ________________________ and______________________ shall share equally in the following expenses and costs:

(a) property taxes;
(b) strata fees;
(c) hydro, cable, and telephone;
(d) house insurance;
(e) groceries; and
(f) capital expenses, such as repairs and extra strata expenses.

OR

(Different payments)

28. Each Party shall be responsible only for those payments listed below beside which his or her initials appear:

property taxes	______	house insurance	______
strata fees	______	groceries	______
hydro, cable, and telephone	______	capital expenses, such as repairs and extra strata expenses	______

(Equal payments)

29. The Parties shall share equally the cost of all utilities, and non-capital repairs as necessary for the general upkeep of the Property and fixtures therein and each shall pay ONE-HALF (1/2) of such costs as and when they become due and owing.

OR

(Payments in different amounts)

29. The Parties shall share in the cost of all utilities and non-capital repairs as necessary for the general upkeep of the Property and fixtures therein as follows:_____________________ shall pay_______% and_______________________ shall pay______% of such costs as and when they become due and owing.

30. The Parties agree that no major expense, including renovation, repair, and redecoration, shall be incurred, unless otherwise mutually agreed; save and except in the case of an emergency when immediate steps must be taken to ensure the safety of the Property.

DEFAULTS

31. In the event that either Party shall fail to pay any or all of his or her payments as set out in this Agreement, such default shall be covered by the other Party, and all monies, costs, and obligations outstanding, together with interest at the prevailing bank lending interest rate accrued thereon, shall be deducted from the share in the net sale proceeds of the defaulting Party and the sum so deducted shall be used to reimburse the other Party for her or his outlay and expenses in respect of the default.

__________ __________

32. In the event that the share in the net sale proceeds of the defaulting Party as set out herein is not sufficient to satisfy the outstanding amount owing, together with accrued interest, he or she shall continue to be responsible for such default and shall be held liable to indemnify and save the other Party harmless from all costs, outlays, actions, and claims arising from the said default.

33. All defaults in payments and costs shall accrue interest at the prevailing bank lending interest rate at the time of the default until such payments and costs are paid in full.

OTHER PROPERTY, ASSETS, AND LIABILITIES

(Separate property) 34. EXCEPT AS SPECIFICALLY PROVIDED HEREIN, property brought into the relationship by each of the Parties, and specifically those major assets set out in Schedule A and Schedule B hereto or purchased solely by one Party during the relationship, shall remain the sole property of such Party, and____________________ and____________________ hereby agree that they shall remain separate as to personal and real property with respect to all interest in personal and real property of either as the same existed prior to their relationship.

OR

(Equal shares) 34. EXCEPT AS SPECIFICALLY PROVIDED HEREIN, property brought into the relationship by each of the Parties, including those major assets set out in Schedule A and Schedule B hereto or purchased solely by one Party during the relationship shall be the joint property of both Parties, held in equal share. However, any and all property inherited by either Party from that Party's family shall remain that Party's separate property, with no right or entitlement to that property to the non-inheriting spouse.

(Separate liability) 35. Liabilities incurred by each of the Parties shall remain the personal liability of such Party.

OR

(Joint liability) 35. Liabilities incurred by either Party during the period of cohabitation are the joint obligation and responsibility of both Parties. If either Party wishes to contract for a debt of more than $__________._______, the other Party must be told in advance and must give his/her consent in writing for that specific obligation before it is incurred.

36. Property and assets acquired jointly by the Parties shall be shared equally between the Parties as joint tenants.

37. In the event of the termination of the relationship, for whatever reason, ___________________________ and_____________________ agree to divide such joint property and joint assets in an equitable and amicable manner. Should such amicable division not be possible or practicable, the Parties agree to submit the decision respecting the division of such joint property and assets to arbitration in accordance with Paragraph 47 hereof.

CHILDREN

38. It is the intention of both Parties not to conceive a child within_________ (_______) years from the date of this agreement.

___________ ___________

39. The Parties agree not to have more than________ (________) children in this relationship.

40. The children born in this relationship will have the surname________________________.

41. The children born to____________________ in any previous relationship will continue to be the sole responsibility of__________________________________ unless custody changes to____________________, in which case the next paragraph will apply to those children equally.

42. (a) The Parties agree that they will each be jointly and equally responsible for the financial, physical, and emotional upbringing, care, and support of their children. As much as possible, the Parties will each put in equal time, energy, and resources to the emotional, mental, and physical well-being of their children.

(b) If at any point it is not possible for the Parties each to make an equal contribution, the Parties will negotiate and agree on the terms and length of time for the unequal contribution.

(No religion) 43. The Parties acknowledge that they are not followers of any religion or religious organization. If for any reason either of the Parties wishes the children to participate in any religion, the other must agree. If no agreement can be reached, then there will be no participation in any religion by the children.

OR

(Religion specified) 43. The Parties acknowledge that they are followers of the____________________ religion, and it is the intention of both Parties that their children participate in the____________________ religion.

SUPPORT AND MAINTENANCE

(Self-supporting) 44. ________________________ and______________________ hereby agree that they are each able to support and maintain themselves and neither Party shall take action for support and maintenance for themselves now, in the future, or in the event of the termination of the relationship.

OR

(Support obligated) 44. In the event that_____________________ and______________________ decide to live separate and apart, neither Party shall be obligated to support the other unless their relationship lasted a minimum of________ (__________) years and:

(a) the earning capacity of one Party is under a serious financial disadvantage because of the obligations placed upon him or her by the relationship; or

(b) one of the Parties is incapable of reasonably supporting himself or herself because of mental or physical infirmity, illness, or the demands of caring for the children of the relationship.

If either of the situations set out in sub-paragraphs (a) or (b) of section 44 exists, then we agree that the non-incapacited Party will pay___________________ PERCENT (________%) of his or her net yearly income as support to the other Party until the financial disability no longer exists, or for a period of__________ (_____) months/years.

__________ __________

(Note that clauses regarding custody and access may not be enforceable in some provinces.)

45. (a) In the event that____________________ and______________________ decide to live separate and apart and there are dependant children of the relationship, the children will be in the joint custody of both Parties, with their primary residence from the date of separation being with___________________. The Parties will be reasonable in ensuring that___________________ has frequent and regular visits with the children.

(b) If there are dependant children of the relationship at the time of separation, then _________________________________ will continue to live in the family home. _________________________and_______________________ will be responsible for those payments listed below beside which their initials appear:

mortgage payments	_______	house insurance	_______
property taxes	_______	groceries	_______
strata fees	_______	capital expenses, such as repairs and extra strata expenses	_______
hydro, cable, and telephone	_______		

(c) If there are dependent children of the relationship at the time of separation, then _____________________________ shall pay child support in accordance with the Child Support Guidelines, and to that end___________________________ shall provide a copy of his/her tax return and income tax assessment annually to _________________________no later than June 15 each year, until the youngest child ceases to be dependant or attains the age of 21. Child support will be paid by_________________________ by providing______________________ with 12 postdated cheques in the appropriate Guideline table amount, starting the month following the provision to_____________________ of the annual income tax return and assessment.

CANADA PENSION AND OTHER BENEFITS

(No division of pensions)

46. In the event of the termination of the relationship, for whatever reason, the Parties hereto agree that neither Party shall make application for a division of the other Party's unadjusted pensionable earnings pursuant to the Canada Pension Plan Act, R.S.C. 1985, C. C-8 and amendments and regulations thereto, nor for a division of the other Party's pension plan or pension schemes through employment, and each Party shall indemnify and save harmless the other Party from any such division.

OR

(Pensions may be divided)

46. In the event of the termination of the relationship, for whatever reason, save and except for the death of either Party, whereupon it is contemplated that the survivor may apply for any or all benefits on the event of death, the Parties hereto agree to equally divide their unadjusted pensionable earnings pursuant to the Canada Pension Plan Act, R.S.C. 1970, C. C-5 and amendments and regulations thereto, as well as their pension plans or pension schemes through employment.

___________ ___________

CONFLICT RESOLUTION

47. All matters in difference in relation to this Agreement shall be referred to the arbitration of a single arbitrator, if the Parties agree upon ONE (1), otherwise to THREE (3) arbitrators, one to be appointed by each Party and a third to be chosen by the first two named before they enter upon the business of arbitration. The award and determination of such arbitrator or arbitrators, or any TWO (2) of such THREE (3) arbitrators, shall be binding upon the Parties and their respective heirs, executors, administrators, and assigns.

48. The request for arbitration may be made by either Party and shall be in writing and delivered to the other Party.

GENERAL CLAUSES

49. This Agreement is not intended to create a partnership, agency, or joint tenancy. This Agreement does not give any Party the authority or power to act for or undertake any obligations or responsibilities on behalf of the other Party, unless otherwise agreed in writing.

50. This Agreement shall continue to the benefit of and be binding upon the heirs, executors, administrators, and assigns of each of the Parties in the event of the death of either of them.

51. Neither Party shall, without the previous consent in writing of the other Party, assign his or her interest in any jointly acquired property or any part thereof or otherwise encumber his or her interest in and to the jointly acquired property by gift, donation, transfer, or otherwise.

RELEASES

52. The Parties release each other from any claims they may have against each other's separate property by way of a declaration of trust, resulting, constructive or otherwise, other than any claims arising under or to enforce the provisions of this Agreement.

53. The Parties agree to be governed by the terms of this Agreement, and neither Party shall commence an action against the other Party pursuant to any provincial or federal legislation as may be applicable to force a sale of the Property, and each Party shall indemnify and save the other Party harmless from any such actions, claims, and costs thereof.

LEGAL ADVICE, DISCLOSURE, FAIRNESS

54. Each Party acknowledges that she or he has had independent legal advice or has freely waived the right to such independent legal advice; understands her and his respective rights and obligations under this Agreement; is signing this Agreement voluntarily, without fraud, duress, or undue influence; and has affirmed her or his belief that the provisions of this Agreement are adequate to discharge the present and future responsibilities of the Parties and that this contract will not result in circumstances that are unconscionable or unfair to any Party.

AMENDMENTS AND UNDERTAKINGS

55. The Parties may amend any of the terms in this Agreement by a writing signed by them and witnessed and endorsed on this Agreement or attached, and all such amendments shall be followed and have the same force and effect as if they had originally been in and formed part of this Agreement.

__________ __________

56. ________________________ and____________________ shall at all times and upon reasonable request put their signature to all such documents and give all such further assurances and do all such acts required for the purpose of giving effect to the terms, agreements, and provisions contained in this Agreement.

57. This Agreement shall remain in force and effect until the Parties agree in writing to terminate this Agreement.

IN WITNESS WHEREOF____________________ has hereunto set his/her hand and seal at the City of______________________, in the Province/Territory of______________________, on the________ day of________________,_________.

SIGNED, SEALED AND DELIVERED)
by_____________________________)
in the presence of:)

_____________________________) _________________________
Name
_____________________________)
_____________________________)
Address
_____________________________)
Occupation

IN WITNESS WHEREOF____________________ has hereunto set his/her hand and seal at the City of______________________, in the Province/Territory of______________________, on the________ day of________________,_________.

SIGNED, SEALED AND DELIVERED)
by_____________________________)
in the presence of:)

_____________________________) _________________________
Name
_____________________________)
_____________________________)
Address
_____________________________)
Occupation

__________ __________

SCHEDULE A

*Major Assets and Property owned by*________________________________*as his sole property:*

Assets **Value**

Debts and liabilities

__________ __________

SCHEDULE B

Major Assets and Property owned by ______________________________ *as her sole property:*

Assets **Value**

Debts and liabilities

______________ ______________

COHABITATION AGREEMENT FOR SAME-SEX COUPLES

THIS AGREEMENT made in triplicate this_______ day of__________________ 20____

BETWEEN:

____

(hereinafter called "__________________________")
OF THE FIRST PART

AND:

____

(hereinafter called "__________________________")
OF THE SECOND PART

WHEREAS:

A. ____________________________ and____________________________ reside together in a committed relationship.

B. ____________________________ and__________________________ (the "Parties") commenced residing together on or about______________________,________;

C. ____________________________ has______ children of a prior relationship, namely,

____________________________________, born____________________________,

____________________________________, born____________________________,

____________________________________, born____________________________,

OR

C. ____________________________ has no children.

D. ______________________________ was divorced/separated from the father/mother of his/her children on__________________________,_________.

E. ____________________________ has______ children of a prior relationship, namely,

____________________________________, born____________________________,

____________________________________, born____________________________,

____________________________________, born____________________________,

OR

E. ______________________________ has no children.

__________ __________

F. ______________________________ was divorced/separated from the father/mother of his/her children on_________________________,________.

G. ______________________________ has the assets and liabilities outlined in Schedule A hereto and no others.

H. ______________________________ has the assets and liabilities outlined in Schedule B hereto and no others.

I. Any undisclosed assets owned by either party shall be deemed to be a joint asset subject to equal division.

J. The parties are both self-supporting.

K. ______________________________is solely responsible for the support of his/her children, namely,

______________________________________,

______________________________________,

______________________________________,

and receives/does not receive child support from the father/mother of the children.

L. ______________________________is solely responsible for the support of his/her children, namely,

______________________________________,

______________________________________,

______________________________________,

and receives/does not receive child support from the father/mother of the children.

M. The Parties are entering into this Agreement —

(a) to resolve all issues that may arise as to ownership and management of property, real or personal, communal or otherwise, owned or which may hereafter be owned by either of them, jointly or severally;

(b) to determine management of, ownership in, and division of assets during their cohabitation;

(c) to determine management of, ownership in, and division of assets; and

(d) to determine support of the children and each other in the event of separation or termination of their relationship.

N. The Parties intend this Agreement to be the final settlement and release of their respective claims and interests relating to the property set out in this Agreement and claims to maintenance and support.

IN CONSIDERATION of the promises and mutual covenants contained herein, the Parties agree as follows:

__________ __________

1. INTENT OF AGREEMENT

1.1 ________________________________ and ____________________________ separately acknowledge that:

(a) their relationship is tantamount to spousal;

(b) in the course of the relationship, each of them will confer benefits upon the other; benefits conferred by one Party upon the other are gifts, and the making of these gifts does not result in an unjust enrichment of the recipient to the detriment of the donor;

[From among paragraphs (c), (d), (e), and (f), choose those that apply to your situation. Strike through those that do not apply to your situation.]

(Separate property)

(c) neither Party intends to share legal or beneficial ownership of his/her separate property, owned before or acquired after the making of this Agreement, save and except where set out in this Agreement or where the Parties expressly agree in writing; and

(Separate Property)

(d) neither Party shall rely upon the oral expression, or conduct which may suggest the expression, of an intention by one Party to hold property or a portion of property in trust for the other Party.

(Equal shares)

(e) both Parties intend to equally share the legal and beneficial ownership of their separate property, owned before or acquired after the making of this Agreement, save and except where set out in this agreement or where the Parties expressly agree in writing; and

(Equal shares)

(f) all property of whatever kind purchased by either or both Parties while cohabitating will be the joint property of both Parties and is held in equal shares with equal right to its use and enjoyment save and except where set out in this Agreement or where the Parties expressly agree in writing.

1.2 ___________________________________ represents and agrees that all of his/her assets and liabilities as of the date of this Agreement will be accurately listed in a schedule which, upon being initialled by both __________________________ and ______________________________, shall be attached hereto as Schedule A and form part of this Agreement. ____________________ acknowledges that ________________________________ is relying on this representation as to the accuracy of Schedule A.

1.3 ___________________________________ represents and agrees that all of his/her assets and liabilities as of the date of this Agreement will be accurately listed in a schedule which, upon being initialled by both __________________________ and ______________________________, shall be attached hereto as Schedule B and form part of this Agreement. ____________________ acknowledges that ________________________________ is relying on this representation as to the accuracy of Schedule B.

__________ __________

1.4 The Parties each agree that it is their intent that, if the Parties cohabit, this Agreement shall be a full and final settlement of all property issues arising prior to their cohabitation, during their cohabitation, and on the breakdown of their relationship. The Parties each agree that the terms of this Agreement shall survive any separation of the parties.

(Separate property)

1.5 The Parties each agree that it is their intent that, subject only to this Agreement, ____ shall retain the assets listed in Schedule A, and ____________________________________ shall retain the assets listed in Schedule B as his/her sole property hereto in the event of separation and termination of the relationship of the Parties.

OR

(Equal shares)

1.5. The Parties each agree that it is his or her intent that, subject to this Agreement, the assets referred to in Schedule A and Schedule B shall be divided in equal shares if the Parties separate.

2. INTERPRETATION

2.1 Unless otherwise specifically provided herein, the words used in this Agreement shall have the meaning ordinarily applied to such words.

2.2 If any portion of this Agreement is found to be illegal, unenforceable, void, or voidable, each of the remaining items shall remain in full force and effect as a separate contract.

(Name your province of residence)

(State the name of the high court of your province)

2.3 This Agreement shall be interpreted and take effect in accordance with the laws of ____________________________, and the Parties agree that any action concerning or relating to this Agreement in any respect shall be brought in__________________________ and that each agrees to the jurisdiction of the____________________________________ Court for this purpose.

2.4 The section titles in this Agreement are for convenience only and shall not be construed to affect the meanings of the sections so entitled.

3. PROPERTY

(Insert legal description as found in property tax notice)

3.1 ___________________________________ is the registered owner of the property and premises located at____, in the City of________________________, in the Province of _________________________, more legally known and described as:_______________ ____(hereinafter called "the Property") which is the home of_________________________________.

3.2 ____ is and shall remain the sole registered owner of the Property.

[Clauses 3.3 to 3.4 to be used if one Party is to acquire an interest in the Property owned by the other party.]

3.3 ____ purchased the Property on _____________________________________, for________________________________, and the current fair market value is approximately_______________________________.

___________ ___________

3.4 Notwithstanding the above,__________________________ agrees that while he/she and __________________________ cohabit,______________________ shall acquire an interest in the Property on an incremental basis as follows:

(a) __________________________________ shall have sole title to and ownership of _____________ PERCENT (_______%) of the Property in recognition of his/her down payment of $______________________ (the "down payment"), free of any claim by______________________, this being the current equity in the Property;

(b) The remaining_____________ PERCENT (__________%) interest in and to the Property represents the mortgages against the Property in the amount of $________________________, the liability for this share of the Property shall be divided equally between______________________ and__________________;

(c) ______________________'s share of the equity in the Property shall rise as the mortgages are paid down at the rate of____ and_____ PERCENT (_________%) per year, PROVIDED HOWEVER that_______________ shall pay his/her share of the mortgage payments;

(d) ______________________ shall have the option to pay to__________________ a lump sum payment for the purchase of an additional interest in the Property in proportion to the amount of his/her payment, which proportion and additional interest shall be agreed in writing between the Parties and added as an addendum to this Agreement.

4. MORTGAGE

4.1 There is a mortgage/loan/line of credit in the sum of________________________, in the name of____________________, dated___________________________, registered against the Property and held by_____________________, (now referred to in this Agreement simply as the "Mortgage").

4.2 The monthly payment due and owing pursuant to the Mortgage is currently in the amount of____________________ per month, including principal and interest and not including property taxes (now referred to in this Agreement simply as the "the Mortgage Payments").

(Equal payments)

4.3 _______________________ and__________________________ shall share the Mortgage Payments equally, such that each of the Parties pay_____________________________ per month.

OR

(Payments in different amounts)

4.3 The Parties shall share the Mortgage Payments, such that__________________________ shall pay $_____________ (___________________________) and____________________ shall pay $_____________ (___________________________).

4.4 Each Party hereto shall not further encumber the mortgage or transfer his/her interest, whether legal or beneficial, in and to the Property in any way whatsoever.

__________ __________

5. BUY/SELL PROVISIONS

[Clauses 5.1 to 5.9 to be used if both parties have an interest in the Property.]

5.1 If__________________ wishes to sell his/her interest in and to the Property, he/she shall first give written notice of such intention to__________________________, and she/he shall have the first option to purchase the interest of_________________________________ at a price to be determined by a current appraisal of the market value of the property; this option shall remain open for a period of____________ (_____) days from the date of the receipt by______________ ______________________________of the written notice.

5.2 If____________________ wishes to sell her/his interest in the Property, she/he shall first give written notice of such intention to__________________________, and he/she shall have the first option to purchase the interest of______________________ at a price to be determined by a current appraisal of the market value of the Property; which said option shall remain open for a period of______________ (_________) days from the date of the receipt by_________________ of the written notice.

5.3 In the event of the termination of the relationship between____________________ and__________________________, for any reason whatsoever,____________________ shall have the first option to purchase the interest of the other Party at a price to be determined by a current appraisal of the market value of the Property; which said option shall remain open for a period of______________ (________) days from the date of the termination of the relationship.

5.4 In the event that neither of the Parties wishes to exercise his/her option as set out herein or upon the expiry of the option period, the Parties shall list the Property for sale with a Multiple Listing Service at a listing price to be determined by agreement or as set out in Paragraph 5.5 herein, BUT UNDER NO CIRCUMSTANCES shall the Property be sold at a price less than the original purchase price, unless otherwise mutually agreed in writing.

5.5 In the event there is no agreement between the Parties as to the listing price or option purchase price, it shall be set by obtaining THREE (3) independent realtor appraisals and taking an average of the THREE (3) appraisals.

5.6 The fees and costs of the said appraisals of the Property shall be borne equally between the Parties.

5.7 An offer from a bona fide purchaser within__________ PERCENT (_________%) of the listing price shall be accepted by both Parties unless both Parties mutually agree in writing to decline the offer.

5.8 In the event that the Property is sold, the proceeds of the sale shall be applied first to the commission to any real estate agency involved in the sale; second, to any outstanding taxes; third, to any legal or other costs involved in the sale; fourth, to the payment of the Mortgage; fifth, to the payment to________________________ of his/her______________ PERCENT (________%) share of the Property; sixth, to any defaults as may be outstanding to the non-defaulting Party, as set out in Paragraph 7.1 herein.

____________ ____________

5.9 The balance of the sale proceeds shall be divided equally between ____________________ and_____________________________.

6. USAGE OF THE PROPERTY

6.1 _________________________________ and______________________________ shall share equally in the use and occupation of the Property during the course of their relationship.

(Equal payments)

6.2 ____________________________ and____________________________ shall share equally in the following expenses and costs:

(a) property taxes;
(b) strata fees;
(c) hydro, cable, and telephone;
(d) house insurance;
(e) groceries; and
(f) capital expenses, such as repairs and extra strata expenses.

OR

(Different payments)

6.2 Each Party shall be responsible only for those payments listed below beside which his/her initials appear:

property taxes	_______	house insurance	_______
strata fees	_______	groceries	_______
hydro, cable, and telephone	_______	capital expenses, such as repairs and extra strata expenses	_______

(Equal payments)

6.3 The Parties shall share equally the cost of all utilities, and non-capital repairs as necessary for the general upkeep of the Property and fixtures therein and each shall pay ONE-HALF (1/2) of such costs as and when they become due and owing.

OR

(Payments in different amounts)

6.3 The Parties shall share in the cost of all utilities and non-capital repairs as necessary for the general upkeep of the Property and fixtures therein as follows:______________________ shall pay_________% and____________________ shall pay________% of such costs as and when they become due and owing.

6.4 The Parties agree that no major expense, including renovation, repair, and redecoration, shall be incurred, unless otherwise mutually agreed; save and except in the case of an emergency when immediate steps must be taken to ensure the safety of the Property.

[Clause 6.5 to be used if one Party retains ownership of the Property.]

6.5 ____________________________as owner of the property, shall be solely responsible for any and all capital repairs, improvements, and replacements with respect to the Property and the appliances therein.

____________ ____________

7. DEFAULTS

[To be used if one Party retains ownership of the Property.]

7.1 In the event that either Party shall fail to pay any or all of his/her payments as set out in this Agreement, such default shall be covered by the other Party, and all monies, costs, and obligations outstanding together with interest at the prevailing bank lending interest rate accrued thereon shall be deducted or added, as the case may be, to the Settlement Payout to ______________________________ as set out herein.

OR

[To be used if both Parties have an interest in Property.]

7.1 In the event that either Party shall fail to pay any or all of his or her payments as set out in this Agreement, such default shall be covered by the other Party, and all monies, costs, and obligations outstanding, together with interest at the prevailing bank lending interest rate accrued thereon, shall be deducted from the share in the net sale proceeds of the defaulting Party and the sum so deducted shall be used to reimburse the other Party for her or his outlay and expenses in respect of the default.

8. OTHER PROPERTY, ASSETS, AND LIABILITIES

(Separate property)

8.1 Property brought into the relationship by each of the Parties and specifically those assets set out in Schedules A and B hereto or purchased solely by one Party during the relationship shall remain the sole property of such party, and____________________ and________________ hereby agree that they shall remain separate as to personal and real property with respect to all interest in personal and real property of either as the same existed prior to their relationship.

OR

(Equal shares)

8.1 EXCEPT AS SPECIFICALLY PROVIDED HEREIN, property brought into the relationship by each of the Parties, including those major assets set out in Schedule A and Schedule B hereto or purchased solely by one Party during the relationship shall be the joint property of both Parties, held in equal share. However, any and all property inherited by either Party from that Party's family shall remain that Party's separate property, with no right or entitlement to that property to the non-inheriting Party.

(Separate liability)

8.2 Liabilities incurred by each of the Parties shall remain the personal liability of such Party.

OR

(Joint liability)

8.2 Liabilities incurred by either Party during the period of cohabitation are the joint obligation and responsibility of both Parties. If either Party wishes to contract for a debt of more than $_________._______, the other Party must be told in advance and must give his/her consent in writing for that specific obligation before it is incurred.

8.3 Property and assets acquired jointly by the Parties shall be shared equally between the Parties as joint tenants.

____________ ____________

8.4 In the event of the termination of the relationship, for whatever reason, ____________________________ and ______________________________ agree to divide such joint property and joint assets in an equitable and amicable manner. Should such amicable division not be possible or practicable, the Parties agree to submit the decision respecting the division of such joint property and assets to mediation in accordance with Clause 12 hereof.

9. CANADA PENSION OR OTHER PENSION BENEFITS

(No division of pensions)

9.1 In the event of the termination of the relationship, for whatever reason, save and except for the death of either Party, whereupon it is contemplated that the survivor may apply for any or all benefits on the event of death, the Parties hereto agree that neither Party shall make application for a division of the other Party's unadjusted pensionable earnings pursuant to the Canada Pension Plan Act, R.S.C. 1970, C. C-5 and amendments and regulations thereto, nor for a division of the other Party's pension plan or pension schemes through employment, and each Party shall indemnify and save harmless the other Party from any such division.

OR

(Pensions to be divided)

9.1 In the event of the termination of the relationship, for whatever reason, save and except for the death of either Party, whereupon it is contemplated that the survivor may apply for any or all benefits on the event of death, the Parties hereto agree to equally divide their unadjusted pensionable earnings pursuant to the Canada Pension Plan Act, R.S.C. 1970, C. C-5 and amendments and regulations thereto, as well as their pension plans or pension schemes through employment.

10. SUPPORT AND MAINTENANCE

(Self-supporting)

10.1 Both ______________________________ and ____________________________ covenant and agree that they each are self-supporting and shall not claim interim or permanent maintenance from each other now or in the future, and forever discharges and releases each other from all such claims pursuant to any law or statute.

OR

(Support obligated)

10.1 In the event of termination of the Parties' relationship, ______________________________ agrees to pay support and maintenance to ________________________ of $________ (________) per month for________ months/years, or until____________________________________.

10.2 __________________________ acknowledges and agrees that he/she and the father/mother of his/her children, namely,

____,

____,

____,

have the sole obligation for the support of his/her children and that, notwithstanding the close relationship between_________________________ and the children,_________________________ shall not claim interim or permanent child support for the support of the children from ______________________________now or in the future.

____________ ____________

10.3 ______________________________ acknowledges and agrees that he/she and the father/mother of his/her children, namely,

______________________________,

______________________________,

______________________________,

have the sole obligation for the support of his/her children and that, notwithstanding the close relationship between______________________ and the children,______________________ shall not claim interim or permanent child support for the support of the children from ______________________ now or in the future.

11. SEPARATION

[Clauses 11.1 to 11.5 to be used where one Party retains ownership of the Property.]

11.1 IN THE EVENT of separation and termination of the relationship, for whatever reason, save and except for the death of either of the Parties,______________________ shall vacate the Property within THIRTY-ONE (31) days of the date agreed between the Parties as the separation date.

11.2 IN THE FURTHER EVENT that the Parties cannot agree on the separation date, ______________________ shall vacate the Property within THIRTY-ONE (31) days of receipt of written notice by______________________ to vacate the Property.

11.3 IN THE EVENT of separation and termination of the relationship before______________, ______________________ shall pay to______________________ in full recognition of any deprivation______________________ has incurred as a result of his/her contributions to the Property and the family and in full and final settlement of any and all claims arising from the relationship of the Parties, the sum of______________________ DOLLARS ($__________) (hereinafter called "the Settlement Payout") forthwith upon him/her vacating the Property. Such amount is in lieu of any claim for a share in the property or support or maintenance.

11.4 IN THE EVENT of separation and termination of the relationship after, ______________________, and including______________________,______________________ shall pay to______________________in addition to the Settlement Payout, the sum of______________________($____________) per year for every year the relationship continues after______________________. Calculations shall be made *pro rata* on any partial year. Such amount is in lieu of any claim for a share in the property or support or maintenance.

11.5 In addition, the total amount of the Settlement Payout shall be increased by a percentage increase based on the percentage increase, if any, in the Canadian Consumer Price Index for the ______________________ area from the date of this Agreement to the date of separation. Such amount is in lieu of any claim for a share in the property or support or maintenance.

__________ __________

12. CONFLICT RESOLUTION

12.1 If a dispute arises concerning this Agreement, neither of the Parties shall commence court proceedings until the Parties have attempted mediation.

12.2 The Parties shall share equally the costs of mediation.

12.3 The request for mediation may be made by either Party and shall be in writing and delivered to the other Party.

13. GENERAL CLAUSES

13.1 This Agreement is not intended to create a partnership, agency, or joint tenancy. This Agreement does not give any Party the authority or power to act for or undertake any obligations or responsibilities on behalf of the other Party, unless otherwise agreed in writing.

13.2 This Agreement shall continue to the benefit of and be binding upon the heirs, executors, administrators, and assigns of each of the Parties hereto.

13.3 Neither Party shall, without the previous consent in writing of the other Party, assign his/her interest in any jointly acquired property or any part thereof or otherwise encumber his/her interest in and to the jointly acquired property by gift, donation, transfer, or otherwise.

14. RELEASES

14.1 The Parties hereby release each other from any claims they may have against each other's separate property by way of a declaration of trust, resulting, constructive or otherwise, other than any claims arising under or to enforce the provisions of this Agreement.

15. LEGAL ADVICE, DISCLOSURE, FAIRNESS

15.1 ___________________________ and_________________________ each acknowledge that he/she has had independent legal advice or has freely waived the right to such independent legal advice; understands his/her respective rights and obligations under this Agreement; is signing this Agreement voluntarily, without fraud, duress, or undue influence; and has affirmed his/her belief that the provisions of this Agreement are adequate to discharge the present and future responsibilities of the Parties and that the contract herein will not result in circumstances that are unconscionable or unfair to any Party.

16. AMENDMENTS AND UNDERTAKINGS

16.1 The Parties may amend any of the terms hereof by a writing signed by them and witnessed and endorsed on this Agreement or appended hereto, and all such amendments shall be adhered to and have the same force and effect as if they had originally been embodied in and formed part of this Agreement.

16.2 ___________________________ and______________________________ shall at all times and from time to time hereafter and upon reasonable request execute all such documents and give all such further assurances and do all such acts required for the purpose of giving effect to the covenants, terms, agreements, and provisions contained in this Agreement.

___________ ___________

16.3 This Agreement shall remain in force and effect until the Parties shall agree in writing to terminate this Agreement.

IN WITNESS WHEREOF____________________ has hereunto set his/her hand and seal at the City of______________________, in the Province/Territory of______________________, on the________ day of________________,_________.

SIGNED, SEALED AND DELIVERED)
by______________________________)
in the presence of:)

______________________________) ____________________________
Name
______________________________)
______________________________)
Address
______________________________)
Occupation

IN WITNESS WHEREOF____________________ has hereunto set his/her hand and seal at the City of______________________, in the Province/Territory of______________________, on the________ day of________________,_________.

SIGNED, SEALED AND DELIVERED)
by______________________________)
in the presence of:)

______________________________) ____________________________
Name
______________________________)
______________________________)
Address
______________________________)
Occupation

__________ __________

SCHEDULE A

Major Assets and Property owned by ______________________________ *as his/her sole property:*

Assets **Value**

Debts and liabilities

____________ ____________

SCHEDULE B

*Major Assets and Property owned by*______________________________*as his/her sole property:*

Assets	**Value**

Debts and liabilities

__________ __________

JOINTLY ACQUIRED ASSET AGREEMENT

BETWEEN: ____

____

AND: ____

____

1. ______________________________ (has/have) entered into an agreement with *(a)*______________________________ to purchase a______________________________ at a cost of $______________.

(a) Seller's name

2. The payments of $______________ per______________ are to be made by ______________________ to *(a)*______________ ______________________ on the______________day of each ______________ for______________ months/weeks.

(a) Seller's name

3. Each shall make one-half of the payment to *(a)*______________________ ______________________ on the date or dates such payments are due.

4. Each shall keep a record of all payments made. Such payments are to be made by cheque or money order.

5. If either____ or ______________________________ fails to make a payment, the other has the right to make the complete payment and to have his or her interest in the ______________________ increased.

6. If____ and ______________________________ should separate, and both want to purchase the interest of the other in the______________________, a fair price, which takes into account any outstanding payments and the contribution of each shall be agreed upon and a coin tossed. The winner of the coin toss shall then have the right to buy the loser's interest.

__________ __________

7. If no agreement under paragraph 6 can be reached, the________________________________
________________________________ shall be sold.

8. Each shall be entitled to that percentage of the net proceeds which corresponds to the percentage of the payment he or she made of the total price.

Delete one **OR**

Each shall be entitled to one-half of the net proceeds realized from the sale.

SIGNED, SEALED AND DELIVERED

on the________day of________________,

20_______ in the____________________

of__________________________________

in the Province of____________________

____

in the presence of:

____
Witness's signature

____
Witness's name

____________________________________	________________________________ ***seal***
Address	*Signature*
____________________________________	________________________________
Occupation	*Name*

AND

____
Witness's signature

____
Witness's name

____________________________________	________________________________ ***seal***
Address	*Signature*
____________________________________	________________________________
Occupation	*Name*

SEPARATELY ACQUIRED ASSET AGREEMENT

BETWEEN: ____

____

AND: ____

____

1. ______________________________________ has entered into an agreement with *(a)*______________________________________ to purchase a______________________________________ at a cost of $______________.

(a) Seller's name

2. The payments of $______________ per______________________ are to be made SOLELY by______________________________ to______________________________ on the______________day of each______________ for______________ months/weeks.

3. Both____ and ______________________________________ intend that the ______________________________ shall be owned as the sole and separate property of______________________________________.

4. ____ consents to ____ purchasing said ______________________________________ and to his/her assuming sole responsibility for all payments.

__________ __________

5. ____ gives up all and any claim to the ____ and agrees to consider it the sole and separate property of ____________________________ ______________________________ for all purposes.

SIGNED, SEALED AND DELIVERED

on the_______day of______________,

20______ in the__________________

of_____________________________

in the Province of_________________

____

in the presence of:

____

Witness's signature

____

Witness's name

______________________________ ______________________________ ***seal***

Address *Signature*

______________________________ ______________________________

Occupation *Name*

AND

____

Witness's signature

____

Witness's name

______________________________ ______________________________ ***seal***

Address *Signature*

______________________________ ______________________________

Occupation *Name*